In Your
Own Words

33
Biblical
Themes

*With your
thoughts
and mine*

Jenny,

This
Book
Is
Dedicated
To

YOU.

Hope this encourages you,
+ blesses you,

Dave Hopwood

Start

Most days I post a short, creative, biblical thought on Facebook and Twitter; and from April to June in 2019 I posted a series on some of the great themes in the Bible. Grace, laughter, hope, work, kindness, money... you'll find a different one at the start of each chapter here.

At the same time I had also been scribbling my way through a journal containing readings from *The Message* translation of the Bible.

So I wondered about bringing the two together: my thoughts on some of the great biblical themes, with space for you to add your thoughts on the same themes.

And that's this book. 33 chances to let things out. Feel free to argue, to talk back, to agree, to wonder, to dream, to question, to fear, to doubt, to joke, to praise, to sketch, to dream, to pray, to ask the tough questions. All with your pencil/pen/nail/crayon/twig-dipped-in-tree-sap.

Some of the pages are lined, others blank. Please feel free to do with them what you will. This is a book for doodling, scribbling and drawing. Feel free to wander off the subject if you like. It's all up to you. And may the doing of all that help you pause, think, reflect, be honest... and sense God in all of your muddling.

Doubt

'I believe, help me in my unbelief...'
Mark 9 v 24

> The loss of certainty as life shifts and blurs, and ambiguity beckons, the questions becoming more important than the answers. It's a language we can all speak. A way of making sense of our world when laughter and loss, smiles and sorrow jostle for their place in the same moment. So we may voice these questions, belittling their power, and place them on the same platform as faith.

'They worshipped him, but some doubted.'
Matthew 28 v 16-17

* * *

The disciples stand and stare at the empty space. The space once filled by the one who has lived more than they have ever lived. The one who has felt the bite of nails, and whips and a Roman spear. The one who has torn open a coffin, and a tomb, and made dead men walk again. The one who has scanned a seething crowd of thousands and not batted an eyelid when he heard their stomachs rumbling. The one who slept through the fiercest of storms, and then, his eyes still bleary from his rest, stood up and boomed peace across the grim, deathly waters. So many memories, so many moments never witnessed before, by them or anyone else. And now, the final jaw dropping miracle. The man melting before their eyes. Rising up and slipping from one dimension to another. Gone. Even as they watch, even as they will him to stay and do everything for them. Gone. The final whisper of his life carried away by the gentlest of breezes. And yet, and yet, knowing all of this, knowing he really is the one his

3

stories hinted at all along, knowing the Palm Sunday crowd were surely right, knowing that Herod and Pilate together couldn't hold a candle to his power and authority... yet... yet... some of them doubted. Questions persisting, refusing to stop crowding their cluttered heads. They have seen... and yet they wonder. As is the way with us folks of contradictions. Miracles and muddles. Trust and torment. Courage and questions. And perhaps those first faithful followers hate the doubts that chase the certainty around their minds. Perhaps they shake their heads in a vain attempt to shoo the wonderings away, to tip them out of the nearest ear so that they are gone forever. But it cannot be. And so they trudge back to the city. Trusting and questioning. Belief and unbelief squatting side by side in their souls and bodies. And even as he slips away he is well aware of what he leaves behind. Flawed heroes who will always need his help. He knows. He understands.

Matthew 28 v 16

* * *

Have you ever considered bringing your doubts to God as worship? When the disciples watched Jesus ascending to heaven we are told that they worshipped but some doubted. What an honest appraisal of the situation! And they felt it worth recording in the Bible! We can be worshipping and doubting at the same time. In Psalm 137 (that of the famous disco classic *By The Rivers of Babylon*) their worship includes the line – 'How can we sing of God in a strange place?' Worship is not only about praising God for who he is, it is also about offering God our time and attention, in all kinds of situations.

Have a think about the various elements of your life at the moment, the good and bad, and make a list if you like, then offer them as worship to God. You could write them as a kind of prayer, or just as a list. Have a look at Psalm 137 too, see what an unusual worship song that is...

What do you think?

....

....

....

....

....

....

....

....

....

....

....

....

....

....

....

....

....

....

....

....

....

....

....

Love

'That's the power of love...'

Huey Lewis

> The patience, the kindness, the faithfulness of another. The forgiveness, the willingness to let us start again, try again, even though we may fail again. Someone always with us, through the good and bad, gritty and glorious times, in the froth and the foolishness, in the laughter, hope and tears.

'Love is patient and kind, doesn't give up on us, doesn't look for the cracks and the crud. Believes in us and calls us on.'

1 Corinthians 13

* * *

As the blacksmith hammers away, the metal blows raining down on the sharpening spikes, he has no idea. No idea that these callous bits of iron will one day pin up a three-dimensional, sweating, bleeding, holy mosaic. An image captured for all time, pinned on a craggy wooden canvas, set there so that others can go free. He is not an artist. At least he does not think of himself as such. But he does a good job, takes pride in his work. Makes the best of the vocation he has. Hammers and scorches and blasts in the heat. Time and again. Until his creations satisfy his keen eye. Then the work is passed on. To some who construct and others who tear down. To builders and soldiers. Construction and crucifixion. He has no idea what these nails will hold up right now. Could be a shelter for a family in need. Could be a criminal for the sake of justice. Or an innocent man for the sake of something bigger than justice. But he doesn't know that. He sees glowing spikes emerging as he pummels them. Would not think of them as the channels of ultimate love. Extreme compassion. Total sacrifice. Has no idea how many will be inspired to live and die down the ages, how many will spend themselves and find purpose and love and meaning because of his three nails. He hammers on.

Isaiah 53

* * *

Love gets a bad press. I reckon anyway. We love chocolate and three-minute pop songs and cars and curry and sporting events and movies about people in multi-coloured tights, masks and capes. Nothing wrong with any of the above of course. I just remind myself of an old saying, God made things to be used and people to be loved.

Look up the word and this lot comes tumbling out: an intense feeling of deep affection, e.g. 'babies fill parents with feelings of love'; a great interest and pleasure in something. Synonyms: deep affection, fondness, tenderness, warmth, intimacy, attachment, endearment, liking, weakness, partiality, bent, leaning, proclivity, inclination, disposition. Sex even gets a mention but I won't bore you with that.

The Bible has several words for love – eros, philia, storge. Basically sensual or romantic, family, and sisterly/brotherly friendship. Then there is Agape. Oh yes. And that's a whole other story. The love of God. Love like no other. Love that is hard to define. May you know it, that old letter writer called Paul once told us, even though you can't fully. So a contradictory love then. A love we all need, a love to be known, and a love too big, too endless, too extraordinary to fully know. A tunnel of love that never ends. A love that takes a lifetime to discover and then you've only just started. But also a love that carries great cost. A love that is deeply shocking when you consider how Jesus demonstrated it. Loving, forgiving and accepting so many folks that we might well struggle to love, forgive and accept. Crossing boundaries. Offered to the little and the bad, as well as to the great and the good. Oh yes and to the also-rans and the stragglers, the rebels, mavericks and those not trying hard enough.

A love that picks us up, shakes us down, dusts us off, disturbs us with one hand and comforts with the other. An annoying and heart-warming kind of love. A love that defies description in a few lines like this. A love to be lived more than talked.

When you hear 'love' – what words or phrases come to mind? What do you think about Paul's description in 1 Corinthians 13? Is the bar set too high?

What do you think?

....

....

....

....

....

....

....

....

....

....

....

....

....

Grace

'I once was lost but now am found...'

John Newton

> Gentle, powerful help as heaven touches earth. All of us in a pit and needing a hand to climb out. On a daily basis. Weak strength released to us as the unconquerable son surrenders to those who believe they are the powerful ones. Life unleashed in the hammering of nails and the dawn shifting of a deadly stone.

'You were lost but are found, dead but alive again.'

Luke 15

* * *

The lamb looks up, confused, scratched and grubby. Understanding so little of what is going on here. One minute rushing headlong into a bright new future, the next lost, ditch-bound, sinking in mud and snagged on the claws of strange cruel branches. Going nowhere just when she thought freedom beckoned. And the more she wrestles to tear herself from the dark clutches, the more embroiled she becomes. And so, out of breath and bankrupt of hope she collapses and gives up. Then the distant footstep, and the sound of a shepherd. A voice calling her name. She's really in trouble now. Not only battered by her attempts at escape but she'll surely be punished too. Her name sound again, she looks up, her eyes shrinking back into her head, her body all shakes and terror. A smile as the shepherd reaches down. She has no idea what he is saying but there is warmth in his voice. He has power in his fingers, can somehow work her free of the terrible, demeaning thorns, before she knows it she's in his arms and safe. Carried home through the dark night. He seems

12

undaunted by the muck and the mess she has brought with her now. He's not bothered about keeping clean or dry. He's bothered about finding her.

Luke 15 v 1-7

* * *

'I'm found, not sorted.'

I remember that comment mentioned by someone in a session I was leading a while back.

'I'm found in my lost-ness.'

That's one of mine. A thought that keeps coming back to me. You see, if you are anything like me, there are times when you feel that being a Christian means you must be an expert. In the meaning of life and how to love it perfectly, and that's just for starters.

When, around 1997, I fell apart a bit, one of the most liberating things was to let go of this terrible pressure. I felt like a child again. Not able to have all the answers, or indeed any of them, and not needing to either. I needed something else. A shepherd with dirty hands and muck on his clothes. One who wasn't afraid to snag his skin on the complicated brambles of my contrived life. I wrote this.

Child

I feel like a child again.

I'd been trying to control the planet.

Trying to be what I'm not.

To second-guess the one who began it.

Trying to usurp his authority,

Trying to be the one

Who knows all, sees all, loves all.

But not now. Not me. That's gone.

I still feel lost at times. Feel that all I can do is pause and put myself in the hands of the shepherd. Life is too difficult. Too demanding. And being a Christian can sometimes pile the pressure on. Do you ever feel pressured in this way? Feeling you must change the world? Have all the answers? Be a miracle worker?

There are so many moments in the Bible when folks feel overwhelmed. Gideon can't believe he is being labelled a mighty warrior. An angel visiting Mary tells her not to be afraid. Daniel also gets told not to be afraid, a couple of times actually in chapter 10 of his book, 'Don't be afraid,' the angel said, 'for you are deeply loved by God. Be at peace; take heart and be strong!' (Chapter 10 v 19)

Life can seem daunting. The task ahead a bit of a mountain. But God is always at work, and Jesus knew that and looked to join in with that. To hear God's song and be a part of it. I often feel lost, unable to achieve much of anything. So Jesus's assurance about his father being at work, and those words in Daniel encourage me. And sometimes, often unknowingly, I hope I join in with God's song.

What do you think?

....

....

....

....

....

....

....

....

Trust

'I'll be there for you...'

The Rembrandts

A delicate thing, sometimes robust, sometimes damaged or misused. Currency spent wisely. As we reach for a rock to hold onto, for friendship, purpose, wellbeing, direction. An antidote to destabilising fear. The first faltering steps towards relationship. The key to the door of our heart when that divine knock sounds, when the compassionate, reliable One calls, trusting us to trust him.

'Trust in the Lord with all your heart...'

Proverbs 3 v 5

* * *

He thought it would be like standing on a cliff edge, looking down, his knees knocking out a frantic drumbeat and his face white with chalky horror at the thought of the sickening leap into nothing. Thought it would require every ounce of his strength and courage, his fists balled like undoable knots in a hangman's rope. He's heard a lot about this man, and misunderstood most of it. Expected a harsh critic, a loudmouth with a finger forever jabbing at anyone in his sight line. But no. No frothing, foaming, spitting mouth, no spewing of judgement, no relishing of putdowns for those folks who clearly are not up to the mark. Folks like himself. Instead, a disarming smile, a gaze that shows nothing but interest in him, a voice gentle enough that he has to lean in to catch the two words of invitation. 'Follow me.' No cliff-edge then, no snarled threats, no fingers grabbing for his collar. Just the call to take a step. And to try. To make a few mistakes and do some growing. Before he knows what is happening he's

17

shutting up his moneybox, easing himself out of the toll booth, leaving the line of gaping, crater-mouthed customers. It's happening. He's taking that step of faith, and it doesn't feel like falling. Right now it's like the best feeling in the world. Freedom. Chains shattering. So real that he half expects to hear the sound of clattering irons. But no. Just the noise of his footsteps falling in time with the carpenter from Nazareth. Up and off. A new start.

Mark 2 v 13-15

* * *

It's a tricky and difficult thing. Trust. Though I often sing about giving my all, and trusting with every bit of me, in reality I go up and down, hot and cold. Trusting some days with more of my heart than on other days. I get so easily distracted and fearful. So many things crowd in, crushing the good intentions I have.

Life is full of messages about trusting in ourselves. Every Disney film ever made carries the message – *just believe in yourself and you can do anything*. Really? I'm not so sure. Moses was assured he could do what was asked of him, because God was with him.

Plus we have had our trust damaged in the past by those bearing God's image – i.e. human beings. No wonder we find it difficult at times. Other people have misled and misused us. Embarrassed us, hurt us and let us down. And when the image of God does that it instinctively chips away at our trust in God himself. Whether we like it or not we communicate about God in all kinds of ways throughout each day. Because we are his image – broken, scarred and dusty admittedly – but still made in his image.

However, that also means a stranger can smile at you in a passing moment and make you feel better about life. To slightly misquote the great athlete Eric Liddell, 'Everything we do has the power to draw people a little closer to Jesus, or move them a little further away.'

But, back to trust. How do you find this? The writers of the Psalms seem at ease in expressing trust and the struggle to trust. They live with the contradictions. What do you think about that? Like me, do you find it easier to trust about some things than others? Easier to trust on some days than others? Depending on the various situations and circumstances that you face?

What do you think?

....

....

....

....

....

....

....

....

....

....

....

....

....

....

....

....

....

Money

The heart of it, the driving force, the can't-live-with–can't-live-without-it issue. The engine, or perhaps the oil of society. The servant rather than the master? The means for achieving so much, for passing on so much, for building up and yet... for tearing down too. The currency for change?

'Cry out for insight and understanding. Search for them as you would for lost money or hidden treasure.'

Proverbs 2 v 3-4

'Wisdom or money can get you almost anything, but it's important to know that only wisdom can save your life.'

Ecclesiastes 7 v 12

* * *

He looks at the crowd, so many of them struggling to get by, to feed their families, to pay their taxes, feeling powerless, longing for change. He is aware that his words may shock them, frustrate them, annoy them even. But for some there will be comfort. And hope. He knows they envy the rich, can't understand why they have ended up with so little, when others have so much, desperate to be stronger, happier, free. He clears his throat and speaks. The words fall over the people like dust settling. 'Blessed are the poor, the grieving, the oppressed. God is with you.' The faces stare back at him. Did he really just say that? Are they hearing right? Really? But how can that be? Aren't power and wealth a sign of God's presence and blessing? Isn't it better to be richer and more successful? As if reading their minds he glances towards a small group of Sadducees. The wealthy elite. 'Riches can turn into a curse,' he says. 'Wealth can build a wall between you and God and his people. It can bring you crashing down.'

A few of the Sadducees roll their eyes, sure that he is talking nonsense. Jesus looks back at the crowd.

'God is with you who are longing for change, longing for justice and peace and mercy. Those of you who do what you can every day, even in the small ways, to bring that about.'

Luke 6 v 17-26

* * *

The great I Want. The great I Need.

The money monster. The thing that drives so much darkness. Crime. Trafficking. Drugs. Greed. Job cuts. Envy. Overspending. Cruelty. So much potential for harm in a handful of notes and coins and plastic. Unrighteous mammon Jesus calls it in Luke 16, when he tells of a manager who finds a way to use money to bless others. (There is more on this story later in the *Gratitude* chapter.)

Jesus needed money of course, and worked to earn it. And when he invited four fishermen to follow him he provided a huge catch of fish so they could feed their families while they gave up fishing and came with him for a while. Jesus knows how life works. But he also knows how money can create problems. Problems of poverty and problems of wealth. And shockingly he tells folks, many of whom were on the breadline, that knowing their need of God makes them in some way rich.

When one of his disciples, Joanna, chose to support Jesus and his disciples (we're told in Luke 8 v 3 that many folks gave money to support them), she used money earned by her husband Chuza, who made a darn good living working for Herod. In those dark and grasping corridors of power.

Ruthless King Herod of course had no idea that he was bankrolling the true king. Unrighteous mammon fuelling the kingdom of God as it flooded the streets and gutters of the poor, oppressed, overlooked and broken ones. The people Herod was bleeding dry. Who'd have thought it. *Money can't buy you love*, to misquote a line from the Fab Four. No, but it can be used to change the world for the better. Dangerous stuff, yet full of potential.

Money's not easy to write about. So many folks are in dire need of it, so many Christians in the world are extremely poor. What words come to mind for you when you hear or read that word? What would you want to say to God about money right now? Today? It may differ from what you'd say tomorrow, or next week...

What do you think?

....

....

....

....

....

....

....

....

....

....

....

....

Compassion

'You're my best friend...'

Queen

> Giving up any claim to power and privilege, walking our streets, sitting in our dirt, feeling our fear, suffering our pain. Bringing the smile of God and the hand that reaches out to the lonely and the hurting. Living a gritty and lonely life of wonder, risk, misunderstanding, friendship and kindness.

'He became a humble person, laid aside his glory and moved into our neighbourhood.'

Philippians 2 v 5-11

* * *

The angels gather at the window of heaven. Wipe away a little stardust so they can catch a better look. They are flummoxed, bewildered. How can he be doing this? Why? What's the point? They recall the days of gleaming wonder and fabulous parties. The celebrations and laughter. The sumptuous feasts and splendid songs. What's he doing down there? Standing in the gutter, near that widow in rags, putting his hands on that long, empty, battered box. Everyone looks so sad down there. So lost, so empty. The angels don't realise it but they're holding their breath now, their faces frowning masks as they stare. Then suddenly the whole bunch of them jump. Leap in the air. The shock of it! That box wasn't empty at all. A body just sat up in it. And now the woman in rags isn't crying, she's laughing and hugging the body. And falling on her knees holding Jesus's feet. Now everyone down there is laughing and hugging. No more sadness. Not for now anyway. The thing looks like something of a street party. Only a pale shadow of the dos they have up here, but still. Jesus is clearly enjoying it. One of the angels wipes away a stray tear. Perhaps that's why he's gone down there, maybe that's why he's let go of all the great stuff up here. To bring a little bit of heaven to that grizzled planet. It's still mind-bending to the angels, but maybe that's what's going on.

Luke 7 v 11-17

* * *

Jesus gave up so much for us. And not begrudgingly. He and his father were pleased to set this mission going. This unique planet-changing, universe-shifting adventure. God is love we're told twice in 1 John 4. It's his nature to reach out, to welcome, to embody compassion. And this little tale of a funeral disrupted sums it up. This woman has lost all the men in her life, and in those days would end up with nothing. So Jesus resurrected her and her boy. Was moved by her plight and did something.

Unconditional love is a language we have never quite mastered. A country we can see on the horizon, and have only ever made vain attempts to reach. Perhaps some have managed it for short visits. But in general we wrestle with this notion.

Why would you give up heaven? Safety, peace, satisfaction, fulfilment, harmony. All those things and way, way more. Why set those aside to visit a bunch of folks who struggle to care for each other, who snap too easily, whose motives are always mixed. And to face so much conflict, abuse, rejection and torment? 'Greater love has no one than to lay down their life.' And so you did, not just talking about it, but living it, and dying it. Compassion fuelling your every step, your every move.

My heart is so often darkened by personal preference and self-preservation. Why wouldn't it be? I'm human. We all are. And you, Lord, understand that. In your compassion you get that. And still you call me on, to follow, each day. To shadow you, to poorly imitate your selfless living.

27

Even if the day before has been a shambles, and the day before that even more so. You continue to invite me each morning to start again. To follow you, to look for your footsteps and place my feet in them. Thank you for not giving up on me. Thank you that compassion is not only about dying for the universe, but dying for *my universe*.

What do you think?

....

....

....

....

....

....

....

....

....

....

....

....

....

....

....

....

....

Calling

'All we have to decide is what to do with the time given to us...'

Gandalf

To know our purpose, our place in life. To no longer grab at the advertised straw to build our feeble, flawed monuments. To be able to wash feet, knowing the world is ours, a gift, a chance to shine each in our own small ways. Appreciation ousting envy, gratefulness supplanting selfish ambition. A tough call, a moment by moment deciding.

'Are you tired? Worn out? Burned out on religion? Come to me. Get away with me and you'll recover your life. I'll show you how to take a real rest. Walk with me and work with me – watch how I do it. Learn the unforced rhythms of grace. I won't lay anything heavy or ill-fitting on you. Keep company with me and you'll learn to live freely and lightly.'

Matthew 11 v 28-30

* * *

Shepherdless

So many, so shepherdless, so often.
He wanders out of the bookie's
His pockets lighter,
They make their tattooed way,
Saunter past, phones in hand.
She sits on the bench,
Straight-faced, staring,
They perch in a line,

31

Cans in hand, smiling.
They cuddle their coffees.
Wondering, faces frowned.
Neon lights flicker a welcome,
In a balloony fairground,
All floss and prizes,
A carpet of fag ends,
Dry lipstick marked signs of life.
And singing in the Sunday churches,
Some knowing why, others not,
Sheep without a shepherd.
Us. Me and you.
He had mercy on them,
Saw the people wandering,
And his heart was moved.
He loved them to death.

* * *

I wrote this little attempt at a poem when I was wandering around a town not too long ago. Found a patch of grass in a park and scribbled in my notebook. Do you ever get those moments, when you look at normal life and see the hunger, the longing for something more. I sometimes think that cigarette smoke is like incense, floating up to God, a silent prayer, a smoky longing for satisfaction. Got something more. I think ultimately that is the call of God on our lives. To follow him and find out more of what living is really all about. Because at the end of the day Jesus is not about religion, or a mission, he is about life. He came to bring life. He said he *was* life.

I love these words from Matthew 11 as written in Eugene Peterson's *The Message* version of the Bible. So freeing, like a glass of cool, cool water or beer, on a stressy, pressured, hot, melting tarmac sort of day. Or the feeling you first get when you sit down and put your feet up after hours of having to keep on going, going, going. The problem with Christianity is that it sometimes feels as if it is about challenge after challenge after challenge. Try harder, be better, live differently. And when we think of the word *Calling* that can make us think of more stuff we're supposed to do.

But this passage is a big part of the calling we have to follow Jesus. To be refreshed. Jesus was big on telling folks that those who follow him would drink living water and it would be spilling out of them and getting others wet. It was his offer to a hurting woman at a well in John 4.

Later he even misquoted the Old Testament to make the point. In John chapter 7, at one of the festivals, Jesus boomed in a loud voice about how the scriptures proclaimed that those who came to him would have living water gushing out of them. Except it doesn't. Hunt high and low in those ancient pages and you won't find that reference.

There are of course similar writings, like Isaiah sounding off, in chapter 55 of his book, telling folks to come and get free drinks that satisfy. Living water coming to us free. Uplifting, refreshing, helping us shake off the nonsense of religion and niceness.

When I recently saw the film *Captain Underpants* I loved it so much, and laughed so hard, that when I came out of the cinema I wanted to tell others how good I felt. I guess it's something like that. A natural outpouring of stuff. Actions and/or words, depending on who we are.

What do you think?

....

....

....

Death

'What we do in life echoes in eternity...'

Gladiator

> The sting ripped out on that rock-sliding dawn. The hope of another sun rising as a slaughtered son stepped free, the shackles broken now. A new birth possible. The end no longer the end. But a new dawn on offer to us all. The offer of a fresh start and an eternal destiny. For us.

'Death, where is your victory, your sting now?'

1 Corinthians 15 v 55

* * *

Jesus wakes, stirs, stands and stretches. He walks out into the new morning. The world seems fresh to him. Alive. Rejuvenated. He smiles to himself. He has seen many new mornings in his time. As a boy he loved hurling himself into the day, watching the sun rise, running the streets looking for any other early birds. Savouring the air of a new day he feels a little like this now. A new day. Fresh air. And he's looking for any early risers. No doubt one or two will be here soon. He looks around for a place to hide. Spots a secluded spot and makes for it. Smiles again. A new day like no other day. A resurrection morning.

John 20

* * *

Imagine a baby in a womb, growing little by little. Safe in its environment. Being fed and nurtured. Now imagine trying to tell that unborn child about the world it is about to enter. It couldn't fathom it, could it? An environment so different, so strange, so alien, compared to the world it currently inhabits.

Someone recently used this image to describe our entry into the next world. We're like that child. We live in this environment, function in certain ways. How could we really grasp what a new world will be like?

Jesus struggled himself to give us glimpses, saying it was a bit like a good shepherd, a persistent woman, a place where talents are valued and rewarded, a place where everyone is treated well. A bit like a place that is like this world, yet not.

In Revelation 21 John saw a vision of a world where tears would be dried, hearts mended, disappointment upturned. God always present, and death nowhere to be seen. John took his lead from Isaiah, who saw the same.

Death continues to be the great unknown. And the debates continue about what is beyond. It is heart-breaking for those left behind, yet for the travellers crossing the border... well, one thing is for sure, we know that Jesus has walked that way ahead of us. Clearing the path, signposting, lighting our next step. That resurrection morning was way more than another day dawning. It was the start of a new kind of life, a new way of being, and a portal opening from this world to the next.

It is often said that we live with the now and the not yet. Caught between two worlds. Which may be why there are so many ideas and theories about what is coming next. I have just written a piece called The Living Dead (it's on my website at dave@davehopwood.com). I wrote it for Halloween, about a group of bodies climbing out of graves and scaring the local villagers. The twist? It is Easter Sunday morning and these folks were resurrected (Matthew 27 v 52 tells us) when Jesus died. A sign, a foretaste of the resurrection life to come. A new start for us all. Often hard to imagine or grasp right now. But the signs are there to encourage us on.

What do you think?

....

....

....

....

....

....

....

....

....

....

....

....

....

....

....

....

....

....

....

....

....

....

Vulnerability

'You think that I'm strong, you're wrong...'

Robbie Williams

To be open to be known for who we are, in a world of masks and jeopardy. When so much is at stake. To take occasional brief windows of time... to show ourselves, to move out from behind our rocks and fig leaves. And to discover that the fresh air of our honesty helps others breathe a little more freely too. Discovering a little more of the truth that frees us.

'This High priest of ours, this Jesus of Nazareth, can understand our weaknesses...'

Hebrews 4 v 15

* * *

She dances beautifully. Like silk floating in the breeze. Graceful. Effortless. Captivating. The audience watches with bated breath, having never quite seen this before. Such shapes and outlines, as if she is weightless at times. Unfettered by gravity. A dancer from another world, someone not constrained like the rest of the mere mortals around. Apart from her, no one moves. They dare not break the moment, dare not shatter the perfection. This alone was worth coming for, forget the food and drink and the surrounding opulence. Forget the kudos of being on the guest list. This is what everyone will remember afterwards. This will be the talk on everyone's lips tomorrow. Or so they think right now. The music eases to a close, the girl sways and twists and glides to a finish. A moment of stillness then the room explodes as thunderous applause breaks the silence. The girl straightens, smiles and bows. Then runs to Herod and asks for John the Baptist's head on a plate.

Matthew 14

* * *

Jesus must have felt raw the day he heard. His cousin murdered. It seemed for a while as if Herod was happy to keep John in chains, a kind of holy court jester. Providing morbidly curious entertainment whenever Herod chose to go and see him and hear John fearlessly challenge him about the judgement he was facing.

But now this. The news of a death in his family. The shock of what is waiting down the line for him. Matthew tells us that Jesus takes some time out to be alone. Goes off in a boat. No doubt needing to grieve, and to talk to his father about what this means. Before long he will be surrounded by thousands of people chewing on miraculous bread, and no doubt John's death will have slipped to the back of his mind. But for now he needs to face it head on. Looking loss full in the face. Knowing pain and mourning. Blessed are those who grieve, he had recently said. God is with them.

Day after day Jesus faced conflict and questioning. Powerful folks coming at him trying to slam him down and put him out of action. To sideline and wrong-foot him. And those who loved him often misunderstood him, as well as demanding a huge amount of his time. Yet somehow, incredibly, Jesus remained open to folks. He didn't shut off, he didn't close down. He was able to keep on meeting folks, keep on being open to all those who came his way. No doubt his times alone with his father gave him strength and focus for all he was doing.

Jesus was nothing if not vulnerable. You got what you saw. He didn't play those social games, and he constantly urged his friends to do the same. To avoid one-upmanship. To remove the masks and the need to make ourselves look a little better by making others look a little worse. Of

41

course this is risky and dangerous stuff. To not play the expected games, to show a little bit more of our true selves can invite ridicule from others. So perhaps we need to pick our moments carefully. Jesus admitted he used parables to cover up some of his true identity, to avoid the pearls of his life being trampled by all kinds of swine. But there is no doubt, that in the right situation, truth can set us and others free.

I like the moment in the Last Supper, in John 14, where Thomas pipes up and admits he doesn't understand what is going on. Not longer after Philip and Judas also join in. I can't help thinking that Thomas's honesty, perhaps learned from being around Jesus, liberated two of the others to tell the truth a little more. Attending Christian meetings can make this difficult too. The peer pressure to appear to be experts at the faith can hold us back. And surely Jesus would never want that. He's not looking for public experts. Just flawed followers.

What do you think?

....

....

....

....

....

....

....

....

....

....

....

Perseverance

Another mountain, another long day. Another same old dull mission, lack of purpose locks us in, crowds out any sense of direction. Why? When? How long? A trinity of questions loom like clouds blocking out any light. Yet another trinity urges us on. As it has urged so many others, on so many dull thankless days. Alongside us, with us in our trudgery.

* * *

An injured teenager was wandering across a desert, lost and wounded and far from home. She crept into a cave to spend the night, nestled her head onto a rock and settled down to sleep. As she tried to get comfortable her foot kicked against something. She sat up and looked. There was a little tarnished metal box. She picked it up. Hmm, an old satnav. Way past its best. She took it and shook it. Surprisingly it sparked a little. She looked at the dirty scratched screen and rubbed at it a little. There was a second much bigger spark and a cloud of turquoise smoke seeped into the cave and formed into the body of a small genie.

'Who are you?' said the teenager.

'You mean it's not obvious?' said the satnav genie. 'I'm a satnav genie.' And the voice, it must be said, did sound like a typical satnav voice.

'Can you get me home?' asked the teenager.

'I can grant you one wish,' said the turquoise genie.

'Only one?'

'Inflation my friend. And let's face it, thirty seconds ago you were looking at no wishes at all.'

The teenager frowned and thought. The genie meanwhile roamed around the cave, sniffing at various bits of junk and litter that were discarded there.

'I could wish for my wound to be healed,' said the teenager.

'Fine,' said the genie, about to snap his smoky fingers.

'Hang on!' said the teenager. 'I could wish to be back home.'

'Fine,' said the genie, about to snap his smoky fingers.

'Hang on…' said the teenager.

'Oh for goodness sake! Make your mind up.'

A pause. Then,

'I want a mate.'

'What?'

The teenager nodded.

'I want to make this journey with someone else. Someone like me, someone who gets me. Can you do that?'

The turquoise genie snapped his fingers and two things happened. He turned back to smoke and shrank back into the satnav, and in his place stood another teenager. Also lost, wounded and frowning.

* * *

She could have asked to be healed, but then she'd still be travelling alone, and maybe loneliness was a deeper wound for the teenager. Could have asked to be magicked straight home, but maybe there were bits of the journey that she was starting to enjoy, maybe there were discoveries to be made in the travelling of this adventure. She could have asked for a map... but what she really wanted in the end, was someone who understands. Someone with her on the journey.

Joan Osborne once sang about a God who was one of us, riding home like a stranger on a bus. Presumably sat amongst the litter, and the discarded newspapers, and the gum pressed to the backs of the seats and the graffiti scrawled between the blackened wads of that gum. Or to put it in John's words, God became human and lived amongst us. And then called us his friends. Not menial servants as was the traditional understanding of people and their gods. But friends, God with us, helping us make our way through this world. Understanding the good and dark days, and the headaches and the sleepless nights, and the good jokes and the bad ones. A God looking rather like us. One who knows what it is to be lonely, frowning and wounded. One who has lived the adventure.

What we most often need in life is support, friendship, those who are on our side. Whether it's for a chat, or moral or practical support, encouragement to keep going, or wise advice. In Jesus, God showed shockingly that he was absolutely on our side. He had chosen us, chosen to be with us. And ever since then that dedication has most often been expressed in the body he has left on earth. This fearful, arguing, untidy, loving and unloving bunch known as Christians. There are so many times when I have sensed God was with me because other human beings expressed that. They helped me to keep going. To not give up. May you know that support today. May you be able to persevere. Today. And tomorrow. And a week on Wednesday. And next month. Etc (I could go on).

What Peter Gabriel's song *Don't Give Up* doesn't mention (it's quoted at the start of this chapter) is that there is another reason. An invisible reason. The writer of Hebrews chapter 12 points it out. We have a history full of flawed heroes looking down on us, spurring us on, folks who wanted to give up at times, folks who got it wrong at times, folks who were very human. Folks who have run the race and finished. And they are saying to us. Don't give up. We made it. So can you. God is with you.

What do you think?

....
....
....
....
....
....
....
....
....
....
....
....
....
....
....

Laughter

'A good laugh can heal a lot of hurts...'
Madeleine L'Engle

That great gift, triggering those healing endorphins within us. An audible smile shared, sometimes giggled, sometimes guffawed. Suppressed in a library or exploding in a moment of side-splitting joy. Mirth ignited by life's unexpected nonsense; or when we take ourselves so seriously we trip over our overly earnest feet. A holy, healing thing.

'May the smile of your face shine on us Lord.'
Numbers 6 v 25

* * *

He brought smiles to so many who had only known frowns. Joy to lives scarred by sadness. Upended the tyranny of hopeless despair with his irrepressible divine joy, on that resurrection morning. Helps us laugh at ourselves, when others would load us with impossible burdens. To smile together even though life can be dark.

Mark 12 v 37b & Acts 3 v 8

* * *

Google the name of Jesus and you find a lot of pictures of the saviour looking serious. I think we cannot help but equate holiness with a straight face. The more earnest the look, the more spiritual the person. And of course there are many very serious moments in the gospel accounts of Jesus. But God created humour. And for good reason. And when Jesus told his thumping good stories people would have laughed. Really laughed. They were full of humour. When he wrong-footed the po-faced religious experts, the unholy public rabble watching would have cheered and smiled and whooped at times. Being around Jesus made you feel good. Especially if religion made you feel bad. The ordinary people heard him gladly, we're told in Mark chapter 12. He made them smile. His stories were funny. Full of unexpected twists and turns that made them laugh and think and banter about the meaning.

Laughter disarms us. There have been many moments when I have been trying to teach our 6-year-old daughter the correct way to behave and she says something which is unexpectedly funny. And I want to laugh. And hug her. And tickle her. And make us both feel better. (I'm not saying disciplining your children is not important, of course.)

I often think about the Last Supper when I am part of a communion service. Quite rightly we are all looking rather sombre. And yet... and yet... the last supper was a party. A celebration remembering slaves set free from Egypt. Full of food and drink and laughter and talk. And Jesus told his mates to do that and remember him. Celebrate him. I'm not in any way wishing to remove the reverence and respect for God and others. But humour is a vital part of life. And of our life in God.

And laughter is healing. When you are struggling, when the day is hard, when you can't work out a way forward... at those times it's wonderful if a friend, or a stranger, can help you laugh.

What do you think?

. . . .

. . . .

. . . .

. . . .

Faith

'These three remain, faith hope and love...'

1 Corinthians 13 v 13

We all have it, all use it each day. Mingled with imagination, mixed in with vision. Seeing what has not yet come to pass, holding on to more than the present moment, more than the visible now. Friendship, each new dawn, that burst of light when we flick a switch. We believe. One of the great three, along with hope and love. Within each of us, tucked away, the capacity to reach beyond ourselves, for more.

'Faith is the confident assurance that what we hope for is going to happen.'

Hebrews 11 v 1

* * *

He walks the street going over things in his head. Retracing his steps, regretting some of what he said. They were just so full of themselves, full of what had happened. Okay, so it was understandable. If true. But it just wasn't fair. Why should they get that and he miss out? What had he done wrong? Clearly he was inferior. Perhaps Jesus was annoyed with him for speaking out at the last supper, admitting that they had no idea where Jesus was off to when he said he was going away. Which was only true, they had no idea what was coming. But perhaps he should have stayed shtum. Kept his mouth shut. Nodded sagely like the others. He just can't do that. It's not his way. Just like he can't merely smile benignly when they tell him they've seen Jesus and he's missed out. 'Oh great!' he might have said. 'You mean you saw a miracle whilst I was out risking my life to get you some food? You mean you

55

now know beyond any doubt that Jesus is alive and well, and I have to settle for a garbled and frankly slightly cocky account from you lot? Oh good! Oh great! I'm so pleased.' It's not fair. It's just not fair. He always suspected he wasn't up to the job, hasn't got enough faith to be a proper disciple. Well this proves it, doesn't it. He'll just go back to the group tonight, one last time, collect his things and then quietly do a runner.

John 20 v 24-29

* * *

Believing and seeing. Thomas's great dilemma in John chapter 20. All his mates had seen and believed. Thomas was miffed. Maybe because everyone was so full of the story, maybe because he felt stupid, maybe because he was disappointed. Or a hundred other reasons. But he refused to believe without some evidence. And when Jesus offered him what he was looking for, the *science bit* if you like, the carpenter added a new beatitude. 'Blessed are all those millions who will believe without seeing.'

And there are plenty of us. Down the ages and across the globe. We never doubt for a second, are full of assurance, never question, never falter, never... oh hang on a minute. What am I talking about? Of course we doubt and question and falter! We're humans. We understand Thomas, more than we might care to admit. Some days we have that confident assurance that what we believe in is true and vital and life-giving and some days we throw the toys out of the playpen and cry for something more solid.

I do anyway. Thank goodness for that ancient art of *picking yourself up and dusting yourself down and starting all over again.* I do it regularly, and it's not to be sniffed at. I can't help wondering if Jesus didn't have one or two moments like this.

Like the time when his friends brought him a boy they couldn't heal, in spite of their best efforts, and he threw his face to the sky and groaned rather loudly. 'How long?'

he said, 'how long do I have to live like this?' He may at that point have been glimpsing the future, the time when faith will not be necessary because God will be living with his people. And the flat tyres of life will be finally fixed.

Till then, we soldier on, or to use Paul's image, we *athlete* on. Sometimes limping, sometimes sprinting, sometimes hobbling, and sometimes lying gasping by the side of the track. And the good news? God understands all these phases, all these hard days, all our doubting and believing.

He really doesn't demand perfect, flawless faith, I'm pretty sure he's more interested in honesty and reality.

What about you?

What do you think?

....
....
....
....
....
....
....
....
....
....
....
....
....
....

Living Water

'Is anyone thirsty? Come and drink. Even if you have no money. Come to me and drink.'

Isaiah 55 v 1

The kind of refreshment that is free to all: rich, poor, weak, strong. Touching those deep places within us that are so hard to reach. The kind of refreshment that leads to a different way of living, a different way of life. Like water bubbling up from a spring in the driest land, the most arid of deserts, an oasis of hope. Water that rises up within each of us, spilling out and refreshing other people and places too.

'If anyone is thirsty, then you can come to me and drink streams of life-giving water.'

John 7 v 37

* * *

Ultimate entrepreneurs Creator Inc. have announced their new radical plan for the future. They say that, in accordance with ancient guidelines and timeless truths, they will be setting in progress a brand new programme of rescue for the universe. This will begin in the form of a baby, born in fragility and squalor, and growing through childhood and puberty, on into adulthood. Having experienced normal life, with all its shades, wonders and difficulties, the figure will then take to the road, demonstrating Creator Inc.'s passion for all those marginalised, shoved down, overlooked and held back. The ultimate purpose of this plan will be displayed in three days of weakness, loss, terror and punishment, before a fresh start sets everything in a new light. Creator Inc. will then be offering shares in their company as a free option to all those longing for change and a new beginning, alongside a manifesto which invites all new shareholders to partake in working for the company. Opposers of this campaign say that it does not go far enough, saying that Creator Inc. should do more to intervene and put everything right. Or at least do something to prove that the company is viable, powerful and actually exists. Creator Inc. has responded to this by inviting all its opponents to come closer and taste and see that, although this plan will not yet set everything right, it is the best way forward for now. Creator Inc. says there **are** future plans for a universal reboot. But only when the time is right.

* * *

Isaiah 55 offers us the unbelievable. They say there is no such thing as a free lunch, but this is an offer of a free life. Not an easy life. But a fulfilling, cherished one. Don't waste your money on all those supposed free lunches, the prophet seems to say, come and try this one. Money not necessary. Kudos not needed. Power and position are irrelevant. Just a hunger and a thirst for something more, something better. Something genuine.

What holds us back? Well, what holds me back? Caution, busyness, distractions, worry that I might be asked to do something I cannot do, or am too scared to do. Peer pressure, fear of commitment. All these kinds of things. Thankfully God is patient, and he keeps on knocking at the door, and nudging me. And he most likely understands that this life we are sharing together will always be a case of one step forward one step back.

There are days when this abundant life crashes in on me and it's the best thing ever, and I wonder why I hold back at other times. But then the other times come and I forget what a wonderful gift is on offer here. I let my doubts and misjudgements dominate yet again.

How about you?

What do you think?

....
....
....
....
....
....
....
....
....
....
....
....
....
....
....
....
....
....
....
....
....
....
....
....
....
....
....

Dancing

'We are set free, like lambs leaping...'

Malachi 4 v 2

Our crushed mourning one day turned into dancing, the shame and pain of our ashes transformed to wonder and joy. Leaping and jumping, twisting and turning, lolloping like no one is watching. Children again, free, forgiven, on the road to somewhere, glimpsing that great open door of dawning new life. A bunch of wrong-footed mavericks dancing in the light, like birds set free from a dark hunter's trap.

'We escaped like a bird from a hunter's trap. The trap is broken, and we are free!'

Psalm 124 v 7

* * *

The crowds line the streets, smiles a mile wide. This is the day and here comes the king. But the watching eyes burst wide. He's... jumping around. In his underwear! He looks ridiculous. Stupid. Exposed. And yet... abandoned too. Happy. Exploding with life. Some of the folks watching are horrified. How can he do this? Cast aside his dignity like this? And from one window a royal woman peers down and curls her lip. But others, the regular folks, the ordinary types, the lower end of things... they're loving it. A king who is not afraid to leap about like this. To celebrate, without pomposity or prudishness. To look a little like them. Some start joining in, doing their own versions of the dance. The feelgood effect travels like a ripple. Passed hand to hand, smile to smile, move to move.

2 Samuel 6 v 12-23

Okay, so you don't have to dance like John Travolta. Or Ginger Rogers. Or Patrick Swayze. Or Darcey Bussell. Or even dance at all. In the film *Gregory's Girl*, Gregory and his friend Susan lie back on the grass and simply make a few arm movements. And that's their dancing. Flicking and twirling their fingers at the sky while they discuss the wonders of gravity. I do like dancing in our house with my 6-year-old daughter Lucy, and also at the right parties, with the lights low. I love flinging myself around the room, hopefully not knocking others senseless in the process. But in other scenarios, say at church when I'm invited to leap about, I often say 'I'm dancing *on the inside.*' It's a useful get-out if you ever need it.

But it's not really about dancing at all, is it? It's about an expression of joy and wonder. And if sitting or standing stock still, with or without a smile on your face, does it for you... then let it be. If it's surfing or skateboarding or high-jumping or knitting or rambling or spinning round on your swivel chair or watching *Strictly*... then let it be. The point is we have something to celebrate. The promise. Another reality. A resurrection shuffle.

We may not feel like celebrating it every day, especially as we drag ourselves yet again like wounded animals from the carnage of our rumpled beds. But hopefully there are glimpses, moments, experiences which remind us that this is not all there is. There's another world, another way, another kind of existence. A bird-set-free-from-a-trap kind of living. And one day, this badly handled planet will be refreshed. And freedom will be the order of the day. So much so that no one will care how anybody dances.

When King David brought the Ark into Jerusalem, the symbol of God's presence, he found he had too many clothes on to really express how good he felt, so he threw most of them off and started dancing. His wife Michal did not like it at all. But she had been mistreated by him. But

David wanted to celebrate, and like Jesus riding on a little donkey years later, he was ready to look a little foolish.

What do you think?

....
....
....
....
....
....
....
....
....
....
....
....
....
....
....
....
....
....
....
....
....
....

Generosity

'A kind gesture can reach a wound that only compassion can heal...'

Steve Maraboli

We give and we get back. Smiles, friendship, strong and kind words, support, energy, a listening ear, a pat on the back, a shot in the arm, a hand on the shoulder. We know what it has meant when others have done the same for us. Rich not because we have much, but because we share so much. A man from Galilee laid a trail and we're doing our best to walk in his footprints.

'Our care for others is the measure of our greatness.'

Luke 9 v 46 (The Living Bible)

* * *

He looks out over the water and wonders. He chews his bottom lip. Stops when he tastes blood. What should he do? Accused by his boss after rumours from a few rivals. So he's a thief now. Really? No one told him. But then the boss never had much of an eye for detail. So he's guilty and must be punished. And now he has twenty-four hours to do something. Anything. Before he finds himself hunched on the pavement hugging his knees. He could of course run off with some of the boss's treasure. Pocket the profit and really be a thief. But another plan is chasing itself around his head. Rather than steal the boss's money, he could *use* it. That appeals to him. And it just might save the day. He could pay a visit to all those poor labourers out there who owe the boss big time... and slash their bills in half. Bless them with a smile and a 'no don't thank me'. Then everyone might just get a blessing. The locals will be able to get by. They'll bless the boss for being a bighearted generous guy. And maybe, just maybe, he'll make a few friends out there for when he's out of work and needs a little help.

Luke 16 v 1-9

* * *

Jesus once told a parable about a dodgy manager who was sacked by his boss for mishandling the company funds. Or at least, that was the rumour going around. So the dodgy manager visits all the poor beleaguered families who owe his boss money and slashes their bills in half. Good news all round. The boss will be praised by all the people, and all the impoverished people are helped with their hard-to-pay bills. Result!

The meaning of the story? Well, one theory is this – the hero of this tale is the cash. It has been used to bless the boss, the manager and the poor people. So, says Jesus, use money well. Whenever possible, let it be a blessing, rather than a curse. And in an age when so much that is wrong is fuelled by the desire for more money, that's radical. The slave trade, the drugs trade, organised crime, so much that hurts people... stems from the chase for cash.

So Jesus tells us to subvert that. Use money, he says. Make something good happen. Bless people. Make life better, not worse. He experienced that kind of blessing himself. Martha and Mary frequently laid on great food and accommodation for him and his friends at their house in Bethany.

My guess is this is not merely about money. It's about all that we have. All our resources. From a smile to a helping hand to a kind word. So, even if it is just a little here and there, Jesus encourages us, be generous with your resources. Make someone's day a little better. With a smile, a pat on the back, a kind word, a bunch of flowers, a meal, a pound, a healthy joke, a text, a letter, a nice surprise. You get the idea.

What do you think?

....
....
....
....
....
....
....
....
....
....
....
....
....
....
....
....
....
....
....
....
....
....
....
....
....
....
....

Gratitude

'Giving thanks with a grateful heart...'

Don Moen

For life, breath, purpose, meaning, encouragement, the strength to put one foot in front of the other, the ability to smile, to lift another up, to taste and see, to develop, to grow, to learn from our mistakes, to keep going, and for those who don't give up on us.

Seeing life with an open heart, as a gift, a precious thing. Our very breath an opportunity. Thankfulness the currency of hope. As if we have been bitten by the kind of bug that brings life, instead of destruction.

'Let the peace of Jesus grip your hearts, and live thankfully.'

Colossians 3 v 15

* * *

She dares not lift up her face. Knows that a dozen pairs of eyes are boring into her. Can feel them drilling into the back of her head. What if this all backfires? What if he misunderstands, doesn't get it, doesn't realise why she is doing this? She blocks out the thoughts and goes on. Wiping away the tears. It's not easy to manipulate her hair, as long as it is, and she's well aware of the inappropriateness of putting herself on show like this. But she has to do it. This Pharisee is hurting the one who's changed her life, deliberately insulting him. And she can't have that. She must honour him, say a public thank you. Her life has turned around. She can start again because of him. Has new purpose, new hope and strength. And she will not let others deride and ridicule him. So she wipes her tears from his feet, smearing away the day's dust. Then she pours on her perfume and kisses his skin as she does so. And when, eventually, she dares look up, she sees him smiling. No judgement in his eyes. Only understanding. And gratitude.

Luke 7 v 36-50

* * *

I have a short film montage of movie characters saying, 'Thank you'. Kevin Costner on his trek to go dancing with wolves, Martin Freeman as he falls in love (actually), Renee Zellweger as Bridget Jones, Helen Mirren as the Queen, Sean Connery as a tough Irish cop with a Scottish accent, Hugh Grant in his typically diffident, Notting Hill kind of way, Harrison Ford, Jim Carrey... even Daniel Craig as 007. All saying thank you. I watch it from time to time and it always makes me feel good, seeing all these superstars saying a whopping merci/gracias/ta.

Gratitude is appealing. Saying thank you to someone can often make their day. I recently read a book about rudeness and apparently the opposite is true of unkindness. Be rude to someone in the morning and the sour aftertaste can loiter in their being all day.

When Jesus healed a bunch of ten folks with leprosy, he was disappointed when only one came back to say a big thank you. I guess he wants to draw gratitude out of us, to weave it through our living. Not easy when blame and criticism are often in the news.

I heard a lovely story on the radio a while back, about a little girl giving her last £5 of birthday money to a homeless person. Unbeknown to the family a neighbour or friend must have seen the event, because the next morning there was an envelope on the little girl's doormat with a £10 note in it and a few lines of encouragement about giving and getting back. I love that story. And I love the DJ for asking for folks to send in good news stories. I think that sometimes thanking others can be like that surprise £10 note, it can lift us as much as it lifts the other person.

What do you think?

....
....
....
....
....
....
....
....
....
....
....
....
....
....
....
....
....
....
....
....
....
....

Hypocrisy

I often struggle with these games, feel the pressure to put on the masks and the costumes in life's public performance. Easy to cast myself in a role, judge and jury of situations, an 'expert' missing the obvious truth of my own frailty and failing. Tricked into thinking I must adopt a look, a walk, a persona for the crowd. But a door has opened, a light continues to shine, a man called Truth has come to set us free. To dissolve our masks with his kind, strong and humble reality.

'Be done with all your hypocrisy and jealousy and backstabbing!'

1 Peter 2 v 1

* * *

The two of them walk slowly to the front, both planning what they must say, preparing their set speeches.

'Oh Lord, I'm glad I'm not like her.'

'Oh Lord I wish I was more like him.'

One eyes the other with disdain, the other looks back with envy. Oh to be a little better at life, she thinks, a little more tidy, more spiritual, more holy, more organised. The first has no such misgivings. He's just glad he's not a mess, not a failure, not a grubby individual. He has nothing but gratitude for being such a good person. Things could not have gone better for him. The other sighs instinctively. There is little hope for her. She turns and slips away, leaving the other to his reverie.

Yikes! This is a tough one. Sometimes the only way to get by is by keeping your head down, hiding your face and waving a well-fashioned mask in the air. Pretending I'm one thing so I can blend in. Be part of the crowd. Accepted and loved by the strangers I find myself currently hanging about with. And some of my reactions are instinctive, I've spent too long framing an expected response to jokes, complaints, outrage and cynicism. I've learned the language and it's hard to unlearn it. Especially in a way that doesn't make me look holier-than-thou or prudish. It's so easy to make myself look better, feel better, by pretending.

Thank you God that you know how to cut through my façade. The way you did when the prodigal came limping home with his speech so he could wangle a job as a servant, or with his brother stomping up and down on the patio with his well-rehearsed indignant outburst. You always know what to say. Or what to do. A hug and a generous welcome for the filthy prodigal, a listening ear and a dose of reality for his insulting older brother.

Please keep on showing me a better way. Gently though, if possible. You know I need it, but fear it too. Your reality. Your liberating truth. Your healing honesty. Help me when I tie myself up in hypocritical knots yet again. When I play the games and keep swapping the masks. And please help me to laugh at myself when I need to, to have enough good humour to embrace the truth.

What do you think?

....

....

....

Questioning

'How long must we sing this song...'

U2

> Why is this the way it is? What is going on? When... what if... how long... the questions tumble from our lips and our living. A great part of our being and our believing. Room to wonder and to wrestle. Songs of honesty, searching and struggle. All a vital part of our faith. Refusing to settle for less, sensing that life is not the way it should be. So we bring our prayers and our praising, laced with longing.

'When will you give Israel back its freedom, wealth and prosperity?'

Acts 1 v 6

* * *

There is so much anticipation in the air, it crackles like static. Jesus eats with them and they can feel the promise drawing ever nearer. Nothing can stop him now, and that means nothing can stop them. Certainly death can't do it. He's already given them a mind-blowing demonstration of what happens when you try and get rid of him that way. The Romans failed, the authorities were impotent. So bring it on now. Let's have the days of King David all over again. Jesus knows what they're thinking. He recalls something he said to Pilate not too long ago.

'My kingdom is not of this world. I'm not like any other leader you have seen before.'

They nod and chew fish. But they still don't get it. James and John both look as if they might burst. They can't wait to be appointed as his right hand ministers in the new government.

'Do you remember me washing your feet?' Jesus asks them and frowns cloud their features.

Peter clears his throat nervously. No one dares say anything. Finally Thomas pipes up, never afraid to speak his mind, is Thomas.

'Is it happening soon then?' he says, leaning forward, 'are you going to take control? Oust the Romans and start this thing properly?'

The rest of the crew all lean forward now too. Mary, Salome, Nathanael, Peter, Matthew, Susanna, John Mark, Andrew, Thaddeus, Joanna.

He smiles at them. 'It will happen soon...'

James laughs and punches his brother's arm.

'But,' Jesus stops the celebrations with an upheld hand, 'not the way you expect. The kingdom is coming. And with power. But not the kind of power you crave.'

'But when will the revolution start?' Salome asks him.

'It's already begun,' he says, 'on that hill, on that dark Friday.'

And so the frowns return, and they sit there confused. Wondering. Chewing fish.

Acts 1 v 6

* * *

The writers of the Bible are honest. They are not afraid to tell it like it is. Heroes make mistakes, disciples say the wrong things, no one is perfect. Apart from Jesus of course. But the saints in those pages are not really saints are they? Not in the sense that we often use the word. They are courageous and fearful. Believing and doubting. Loving and spiteful. And they frequently spit out their questions and demands. The book of Psalms, the hymn book of the Bible, is full of mixed messages. One single song can contain wonder, aspiration, anger, hope and despair. Psalm 5 is an interesting mix.

When the disciples keep meeting Jesus after the resurrection they repeatedly ask him about the one thing on their hearts. When will peace come? When will Israel be restored to the days of power and prosperity? This is their agenda. And they are not afraid to be honest about it. After three years, a crucifixion and a resurrection they are still misreading this thing. As we often do. And the writers of the Bible don't hide that. They offer to us these accounts of the disciples' frustrations and questions.

If you're like me you frequently feel that you need to offer just the good comments to God, that he perhaps cannot take the struggles and doubts and worries. And yet, a part of me knows that it's not about that. So I need these reminders.

Thomas Merton once prayed the following honest prayer:

My Lord,
I've no idea where I'm going.
I don't see the road ahead of me.
I can't know for certain where it will end.
And I don't really know myself.
And the fact that I think I'm following your will
doesn't mean that I'm actually doing so...

Raw stuff eh? Powerful untidy truth.

What do you think?

. . . .
. . . .
. . . .
. . . .
. . . .
. . . .

Exile

When we don't feel our face fits, when we feel like that square peg in that round hole, when discomfort is the wallpaper of our life... exile. When we feel lost and wandering. This world is not our home. We long for something more, something better, have a sense that life should be somehow richer, kinder, more colourful and satisfying.

'Dear brothers and sisters, you are foreigners and aliens here.'

1 Peter 2 v 11

'In that day I will gather together my people who have been exiles, filled with grief. They are weak and far from home...'

Micah 4 v 6-7

* * *

Sarah lifts her face to the sky. She's having one of her *I wish life was just a tad more straightforward* moments. Every day feels like shifting sand. No place to truly call home. She used to complain about life back in Ur. Wanted something more adventurous, less predictable. Well she's got it now. Every day is unpredictable. And she could do with just a little more that is familiar. Especially at her age. And what with being pregnant. She doesn't want to be a nomad, she wants to make a nest. Something permanent. But that's not an option. They are wanderers now. Exiles. Chasing a promise which seems a long way off. Will everything be all right? Will it be worth all this? Will her baby be all right? Will anyone ever recognise what they have done, what she has sacrificed? She sits and cradles her belly in her hand. The baby is kicking. It wants out. Just like her really.

* * *

Modern life is doing me in. I feel more and more out of touch. I can't stand Radio 1 anymore, sadly. I grew up listening to the likes of Tony Blackburn, Simon Bates and Johnnie Walker. I'm not on Instagram. I don't watch *Strictly* or *Love Island*. I can't be bothered watching many of those epic box sets. (In my day we only had three channels in black and white and we were 'appy.)

I'm fed up of the overuse of the words *Legend, Awesome* and *Gamechanger*. I think high-fiving should be outlawed (not least because it often forces the receiver to attempt an awkward mid-air palm-collision when they'd rather just nod and smile). I don't have a bushy beard, piercings or tattoos. And nose rings just dumbfound me. Apologies if you have one. I'm starting to wonder whether the next culturally hip phase will be to chop off a lower leg and get a parrot.

Then there's the proliferation of news. Or rather bad news. I fear that if Brexit doesn't finish me off then climate change will. There is so much to get your head around. And so much that newsreaders tell us we should 'worry about.'

I feel like I'm in a burning building under pressure to somehow put out the fire, when all I want is to find the nearest exit. Being told to worry about stuff isn't much good anyway. All worry does is make us ill and incapacitate our ability to help. Tell me to do something specific and at least I can respond with a 'yes', 'no', 'maybe' or 'I'll do it tomorrow'. Worrying just makes us chew our nails.

Sound like a grumpy old man? I guess so. Certainly on some days, but thankfully not all. I actually believe in being kind and positive and encouraging. I do! I do! Honest! So forgive this outburst, but occasionally you have to blow a gasket, don't you?

Why all this hot air? Well, sometimes we can feel like an exile in our country/city/town/street/back alley. Far from home, or at least, what we used to call home. The one constant in life is change. And it's leaving me behind. I try and keep up. But I'm failing. And I'm feeling as if this world is less my home that it once was, but perhaps I'm just become more aware of a deep truth.

This world, as it is at the moment, was never intended to be our home. The world was never meant to look, smell, taste, sound or feel like this at all. You and I were made for another planet. Not Mars. But a new earth. A fresh earth. A different earth.

In the book of Hebrews the writer points this out. She/he lists a whole bunch of Old Testament heroes and describes them as misfits in the version of life we currently know. They didn't fit in. They were looking for another place, a heavenly homeland, according to Hebrews 11 v 16. Not so much about fleeing this world, but seeing it revamped one day.

So if you have your moments when you feel adrift, cut loose, not really fitting in... remember that once we catch a glimpse of God's vision for the world, we start feeling like exiles in the present way of things.

What do you think?

....

....

....

Value

'You are so much more than what you own, buy or wear...'

From the film *Bobby*

> Like a diamond in the making that no one has ever encountered before, a precious stone, rough around the edges but being daily shaped. Not perfect, but precious. Every life. Not merely a smudge on eternity's page, but a work of art. Crafted. Beheld. Waking, sleeping, moving, stalling, in the dark and the light and the shade.

'The Lord rules over the deep waters.'

Psalm 29 v 10 (Good News version)

* * *

She wonders why she suddenly feels as if the world is closing in. He can't understand why his moods swing and swoop like a kite. They wonder why they react as they do some days. Lashing out at one another, despondent and cynical towards others, losing hope, living a language they just don't understand. Their reactions often sparked by the most unexpected of happenings. Their days abruptly derailed, by the littlest things. A button pushed, and a reaction triggered. And then they find themselves reverting to the old habits again, clinging to the jetsam that makes them feel temporarily safer. Even though they keep vowing to give up those childish ways.

Psalm 139

* * *

I recently came across this verse from Psalm 29 in my Good News bible and it leapt out at me. *The Lord rules over the deep waters.* The Psalm is about the power of God, stronger than creation, or the oceans, or the weather. And the Psalm closes out with this and a verse about God giving us strength and peace.

The Lord rules over the deep waters. The deep places within us. The places we don't understand, perhaps can't articulate, don't even realise they are there. The places which make us react in certain ways. The places which urge us to do good and bad things. The deep places. And God understands this. The Great King. He can open the gates of those places for us.

It may be these deep waters that make us feel worthless at times. Make us do things to prove ourselves, or assert ourselves, or elevate ourselves over others. Prove we are stronger or better or smarter. We may well not understand what goes on at times. But God does. And our true value is found in him.

In John chapter 13 we are told that Jesus knew he'd come from God, was going back to God and had everything in the palm of his hand. Absolute power. And so he crouched down in the dust and washed feet. Not attempting to prove himself, or make himself look humble, or score points with his father. He had no need. He was secure. He knew how valuable and how valued he was, and so he could do the despised job of a gentile slave. I might, perhaps, maybe... have leant over and given Judas's feet a quick rub with a paper towel. But crouch in the grime and the smell and give those feet a decent clean up? I don't think so. I'm better than that. Aren't I? I'm above that. Aren't I?

Philippians chapter 2 features a hymn about the nature of Jesus, about his willingness to give up everything, to make himself humble. To be small. To be ordinary. To be unremarkable. To take unmerited horror and punishment. To die. Not in order to prove a single thing. But because Dave Hopwood is valuable. Created and loved. And worth dying for. As are you. Precious. Cherished. Known and liked and so, so loved.

What do you think?

Purpose

'Get ready, because God is preparing you for something very, very small... because small things change the world.'

Shane Claiborne

The reason for it all, the reason for this day, this hour, this minute. The drive to do the small things and the large, to care, to take an interest, to do the unique things we can do. To know that it all matters. That if no one else sees the good and helpful things, there is one who does. And that is reason enough.

'God puts salt on our lips, to make us thirst for him and his ways.'

St Augustine

* * *

Paul looks at the walls, the bars, the narrow door. Here he is trapped in this cell, no way out. The air is stale and his clothes smell bad. Where's the glory in this? Where's the meaning? The purpose? There are times when all hope seems to slip away, when that Damascus road encounter feels a long way away. Not least at night, in the darkness. But at other times he is able to remind himself why he is here. And remind the guards too. They all know. He has a reason to live now. Beyond stone and chains. Bigger than the small confines of his living space. And the closing in of his mind. He cannot always hold onto it. But he believes his God always holds onto him. And he is grateful for the kindness of others. Kindness which speaks volumes about the compassion of Jesus. He does his best to hold on to this as he runs this uphill race. Some days he is more successful than others. He thinks too of others who are free and still living the life, still proclaiming God in the small and great things they are doing. Not giving up. He is part of that body. He is not alone.

Philippians 1 v 12-19

* * *

I read a version of that quote about salt in Pete Greig's book *Dirty Glory* and it has stayed with me. St Augustine originally said it, and I really like it. I often ask folks what things in life God might use to put divine salt back on our lips, because life keeps washing it off. For me it can be films, books, news stories, songs, radio programmes. Often it is stories in their many forms. For some folks it might be worship songs, or times of silence, or watching the news and feeling urged to pray.

The point is that God will use the things in our lives to remind us of his presence and his ways. And to make us call out for them again. And our response of course will vary drastically. Depending on our personality, experience, strengths and weaknesses. I love that Shane Claiborne quote at the top of the page. For me it's about trying to find small ways to make a difference. To respond to that salt. To pass it on a little to others. To be a tiny saltcellar for God, if you like. I recently came across this quote in Peter Harris's book *Under Bright Wings*, 'We carry on working, not because of a guarantee of success, or a belief that we can change the world, but because it is right to do what we do.'

I actually do hope my small acts will change the world a little, even in the smallest of ways. But I can't know that of course, I just trust the notion and hang on to the idea.

What do you think?

....
....
....
....
....
....
....
....
....
....
....
....
....
....
....
....
....
....
....
....
....
....
....
....
....
....

Kindness

'It is better to be kind than to be right...'

Jamie Buckingham

In a world littered with roadside casualties, every one of us is a Good Samaritan. A currency free yet costly too. So many chances to be kind-hearted, to tip the balance of blame and jostling for power. Offering mercy. As we have received it from a greater Giver. Heaven applauds every single small, strong and grace-filled act.

Be kind to each other, tender-hearted, forgiving one another, just as God through Christ has forgiven you.'

Ephesians 4 v 32

* * *

The woman shuffles. Soon she will run and gasp and laugh and hug people. But she does not know that, cannot imagine that for a single moment right now. She just wants to die. To fade away and not have to battle through life anymore. The last twelve years have sapped every ounce of strength from her. It's too much. With the loss of blood has come the loss of purpose. She wants out. Out, out, out. And then she spots him, or rather, the crush of people around him. And at the exact same moment, for some odd reason, a verse from the Hebrew scriptures slips into her mind. Old Malachi, and his promise. *The sun of righteousness will rise with healing in his wings, wholeness in the very tassels of his clothes.* She has nothing to lose. No dignity left anyway. If she can just find a way to snake through that crowd and for a moment, even a split second, grab at a single tassel on that rabbi's cloak, well, who knows? Maybe something good will come of it. Moving before she can lose courage she hurls herself, like a hungry, wounded jackal towards the crowd. She still can't see his face but can hear his voice now as she disappears amongst the bodies. For a moment she fears that her smell will give her away. But so what. She pushes through. And pushes through. And pushes through. And reaches, and stretches, and strains and grasps. There it is, the tiniest of fragments, and as her fingers make contact a gentle jolt shakes her body. She stops. Blinks. Can't move. Was that a heart attack? Is it too little too late? She stands there, expecting the crowd to move on. But everyone's stopped now. And somewhere, in the background, a kind strong voice is calling to her. Not by name. But somehow she knows. He's looking for her. Is she in trouble for tearing his clothes, did she tug too hard at the tassel? She swallows hard. Resolves to stay put until the throng has moved on. No way is she walking out there in front of this mob. They'll kill her, they'll fear for their own wellbeing. She shouldn't be anywhere near healthy people in her condition. Suddenly the unthinkable happens, the crowd opens up and every face looks back towards her. She can feel the colour rising in her cheeks, prays for the ground to open up. For an earthquake to swallow her. She hides her face, stares at the ground, willing it all to stop. And then she hears him. And his voice is like a song, like an embrace, like two strong arms lifting her up out of this mess. Slowly, very slowly, she lifts her head. His eyes are wide and fixed on her. But there is not a shred of condemnation in them. He smiles and beckons to her. She shuffles forward. He takes her away from the crowd. Tells her about being well now. Tells her she is whole again. And more than this. Loved. Then he does what no one has done in twelve years. He hugs her. And brings her back to life.

Mark 5 v 25-34

* * *

I love this story. This account of someone who has lost everything being found by God. Lifted up and restored and valued. Such kindness. Such kindness. This woman would have been ostracised, pushed away because of her illness. Rejected and reviled. She'd been bleeding for over a decade. Perhaps she'd become a beggar. She might have tried being a prostitute. Whatever, her life had become the worst of train wrecks.

And now this. The man from Nazareth embodying the welcome of God. Lifting her up, putting the pieces of her life back together. Giving her a new start. Looking her in the eyes and showing her that God cares. Not allowing her to slip away thinking he is just another teacher, or miracle worker. He is God's son. And he loves this world.

His is a hard act to follow. And yet, that's exactly what has happened. Jesus has turned to us and said, 'See, that's how it's done. Now off you go, you try bringing God's kindness to others. Don't worry about falling flat on your face. Just take it one step, one day, one heartbeat at a time.'

It's surely both encouraging and terrifying that Jesus should imagine we could follow in his footsteps. Heartening and shocking. Me? Represent Jesus? With all my hang-ups and dysfunctions? Thank goodness the Bible is riven with tales of flawed folks who got it right and wrong and right and wrong. My rollercoaster life is a little like theirs.

How about you?

What do you think?

....

....

....

....

Hope

More than wishful thinking and clutching at straws. Our eyes set on something more than mere matter. Something reliable. A source of strength and direction, a handful of eternal help. Wedged between love and faith, it lasts forever, placed in the One who slipped into despair, wrestled that beast, and lived again to tell the tale.

* * *

They don't yet know it but this is the day they have hoped for, for a long time. At this moment it's still beyond their grasp, still just an idea. But in five minutes all that will have changed. They sit here now, some with their eyes shut, some hunched with their knees pulled up to their chests. Some pacing the room, studying the floor as they go, back and forth, back and forth, like restless lions. Some lift their eyes and stare at the roof. One or two keep looking at the door, checking that it is still locked. One way or another they are all praying. Praying for something to happen. Anything. For change. For a promise to be fulfilled. Suddenly, abruptly, they all freeze. It's too thunderous a sound to miss it. As if a storm is doing its level best to break into the house. John and James clench fists, ready for some kind of fight. Mary stays kneeling but lifts her head and tilts it a little to hear better, while Martha looks around for something to do in response. Everyone waits, a mixture of fear and hope coursing through their veins now. They're not disappointed...

Acts 2

* * *

'These three things remain,' Paul urges us, 'faith, hope and love.' Faith and love are easily definable, but hope? Often hope can be seen as meaning something we wish would happen. 'I hope I win the lottery.' 'I hope I do well in my interview today.' 'I hope I get a new bike from Santa.' And some hopes are like straw-clutching... 'I hope England win the world cup.' Well, we can *hope.*

But that is not what the apostle previously known as Saul means. Hope is surely about holding on to something we know to be true but cannot yet see. If hope can set me free then it must drive me on to do something. Spur me to action. Whether it is praying for change, acting for change, campaigning for change, or all three. If, for example, we hope for an end to injustice then we can be part of the change. We can do more than cross our fingers. Hope can change the way we see life, and the way we live it.

Jesus hauled his dying body all the way up a bleak hill of crucifixion, with a crossbeam biting into his whipped and torn shoulders. Why? Because of the *hope* set before him. He wasn't crossing his fingers that somehow this barbarity would alter things a little. He could see the radical change that was on the way. It wasn't yet a reality, but it was a hope waiting to be born. Perched in life's wings eager to come on stage. In the film *Hidden Figures*, about the group of women who helped put American men in space, one of those women is asked if she is ready to put a man on the moon.

'He's already there,' Catherine Goble replies.

He isn't. But in her mind he is, she can see the result. That hope will drive her on.

'Rebellions are built on hope,' Jyn says in the film *Star Wars: Rogue One.*

She of course means a positive rebellion, against tyranny and oppression. Hope can drive a wedge between us and unjust reality. Between us and lethargy. Between us and cynicism. Between us and accepting the norm when the norm is just plain wrong.

Economist and statistician E. F. Schumacher once said, 'We must do what we conceive to be right and not bother our heads or burden our souls with whether we're going to be successful.'

It may be the case that hope often looks daft to those who cannot grasp it. But that should never deter us. Hope remains and it is a vital gift for overcoming cynicism and despair.

What do you think?

....

....

....

....

....

....

....

....

....

....

....

A Helper

'I will give you a friend, a helper...'

John 16 v 7

No longer alone. An encourager, a comforter, a strengthening presence. A guide, a counsellor, a force for good. A friend who nudges us, shapes us, moves us towards mercy, peace, reality and kindness. So that we may encourage and comfort and strengthen others, with the help we have received.

'Go in the strength you have.'

Judges 6 v 14-16

* * *

That's wrong-footed him now. This towering man in white has upended his reasoning. It's not fair. He's clearly no mighty warrior, no Goliath, not even a David. Doesn't wield a catapult and regularly take the breath from lions and wolves with a flick of his wrist and a sharp stone. In his house he was always the last to speak, and even then he had to yell above the cacophony of everyone else. Was always the last to be heard. Never picked for the sports teams. Too small, too weedy. And when this stranger pitches up with his greeting of, 'Hello there, Big Man...' well he had to look over his shoulder to see who the guy was talking to... expecting to see a knight in shimmering armour loitering behind him. Surely this gleaming figure isn't talking to him? But he is... so he has his excuses lined up. Ready. Like ducks on a shelf. And the man in white just took a pop at every one of them with his little comment. *'Go in the strength you have.'* That's not fair. He wants to go with a few superpowers. Wants to climb walls and jump buildings, breathe fire and turn invisible. At least be good in a fight. And maybe have a hand that turns into an automatic weapon. Or... or... or a blunt instrument. But no. No Supercharged Hammer, or X-ray Vision, not even a cape. Just this muttered command. He wishes he could feel as confident at this angel. Why doesn't this angel go fight the battle. He'd slay a whole kingdom with the look in his eyes. Why not send him. But no. Just... *'Go in the strength you have.'* Oh... and the promise of something else. He could almost have missed it with his head spinning and his heart pounding out a disco beat. *'I will be with you.'* A helper. And no ordinary helper. No minor assistant. No small sidekick. The living God right by his side. The creator of heaven and earth, right there, in step with him.

Judges 6

* * *

Jesus wasn't a control freak. That is pretty obvious. Time and again down the ages he invites folks to work with him who are clearly going to muddy the waters. And, flipping back in time for a moment, just as he's conquered death and started a whole new work of redemption he ups and offs and leaves the work in the hands of a group of bumbling men and women. Er... what's your plan B Jesus? There isn't one.

So here am I now, writing this book and fumbling for phrases to pass on the good news started by Jesus. Boy do I need a helper. If God doesn't take these words and make something more of them then I'm stuck. My goose is well and truly cooked. I recently started designing some encouragement cards. I was inspired by the story of the mayor of Bogota, Antanas Mockus, who back in 2001 changed his city with, among other things, thousands of encouraging *thumbs up* cards. So I thought I'd nick his idea and I got the following cards printed.

When I go out speaking these days I put them out and invite folks to take a couple and pass them on to anyone who might need encouragement at the moment. From time to time I get feedback and it's so good to hear how the cards are helping people. One time I even got an email from a church in France! A friend had taken one over the water and the folks in that church liked the idea and did their own French version! I tell you this not to big myself up – this was really nothing to do with me. I just designed a card and stuck three lines on it, and it's as if God then went, 'Right Dave, now I can do something much bigger with that idea.'

The Helper took my three lines of text and morphed it into something that is making a difference for folks. I'm so grateful, I really am, because I often wonder if I'm doing much good at all in this world. Probably like so many others wonder at times.

In the movie *A Star is Born*, when massively successful Jack invites reluctant unknown singer Ali on stage to sing her new song with him, he tells her this key line: 'I'm going to sing it anyway, all you have to do is trust me and join in.' That line has really impacted me, because Jesus talked of the way he joined in with what his father was already doing. God is out there, already singing his song of help and rescue and kindness and courage, and he's asking me to join in. And he's asking you too. And what has happened with these little encouragement cards has given me a glimpse of that. What's interesting about this moment in the film *A Star is Born,* is that the song is Ali's song. She wrote it. It's something of her. Jack is not imposing one of his songs onto Ali, instead he has taken her song and made it much bigger than she ever expected.

Who knows what God can do with the things we bring? The spiritual and 'unspiritual' bits of ourselves. The gifts and talents and strengths and weaknesses we have. The life we've lived and experiences we've gone through. All and any of these can be offered to God as we join in with his work.

What do you think?

....
....
....
....
....
....
....
....
....
....
....
....
....
....

Work

'Work? Really? Again? Didn't I just do that yesterday...'

Anonymous

So quickly life's chores and pressures and achievements weigh heavy on us, the burden of so many thankless tasks. The clock-on-clock-off nature of what must be done. The sad fact that gifts and talents and abilities get buried in the scramble to survive. In the mystery of a long-lost garden labouring was once about achievement and creativity and satisfaction. May we still receive glimpses of this. Reminded that all we do is known and valued. And that one day there'll be an endless future when work will be once more treasured, joyful and forever fruitful.

* * *

He picks up the wood and studies it. Might just do the job. His father could make it do the job. When he was around. When he had breath and life and skill in his fingers. His father could do pretty much anything. Including raising a boisterous family of five boys and four girls. He could do with the old man now. Here, advising him about this tricky piece of craftsmanship. He starts work on the wood then blinks as a speck of sawdust nestles in the corner of his eye. He tweaks at it with his thumb. That's when he hears it. The sound of hooves. No one has horses like that round here. Too poor. So he knows. He learned that sound a long time ago. The thundering noise grows. He steps outside, looks beyond the village, sees the growing plumes of dust. Nods at the other men who have paused their work, gardening, farming, building, raising their kids. And talking of kids there's a throng of them too. Not still and tense like their old men, but haggling for a better view, wrestling, pretending to ride their own horses, trying to outdo each other. And all the while the riders draw closer. They have faces now. And helmets and weapons and scowls. The locals instinctively pull back from the road, don't want to be in the way of that lot when they come through.

'Is it Ben?' someone asks.

They've suspected for a while. Wondered. Tried to caution their neighbour about his actions and grand claims. Everyone knows what happens and Ben should know better. And still they come. Close now. The folks can smell the horses and the dust. One man looks around and starts towards Ben's house, but his wife pulls him back. Don't be stupid. Don't do anything that might alert the invaders. They ride in. Four of them. All might and arrogance and sweat. One of them dismounts and strides straight up to Jesus. Perhaps senses a figure of authority there. He spits Ben's name at him. Jesus stares back, sees more than a speck of sawdust clouding his enemy's eye.

'Would you like a drink?' Jesus asks, 'we have water. Fresh.'

The officer eyes him. They are both aware that the Roman's original question hangs in the air, unanswered. The soldier nods and Jesus goes for a cup. By the time he is back the men have saddled up again, and this time Ben is sitting behind one of the others. Dishevelled. Bruised. Secured. Going away. Jesus passes the cup to the officer who drinks it down in one and tosses the cup back.

'Why d'you give them water?'

It's Mary, his mother, standing beside him now, watching as the men ride off, clutching her shawl to herself for comfort.

'He looked thirsty,' Jesus tells her.

'Pa! I hate him. I hate them all. You know we'll never see Ben again. Thank goodness he had no wife or child.' She eyes her son carefully. 'You must take care when they come around,' she says to Jesus. 'Don't want you on the back of that horse. You have things to do.'

He smiles at her and nods. He does have things to do. Building, carpentry. His dad's business. And one day, in a while... his father's business too. He goes back to work.

Luke 2 v 40

* * *

It's easy to forget that Jesus worked hard for many years. First with his dad then on his own. Maybe with his brothers too. Day in, day out. Getting up. Honing his craft. Dealing with customers. Somehow surviving high Roman taxation. Providing for his mother and his four brothers and several sisters. Slaving away. No doubt having good days and bad. Ups and downs. The Jesus of those eighteen years between visiting the temple at age twelve and starting his Messianic work at age thirty. It's a long time isn't it? Eighteen years. I was working in a cinema eighteen years ago. Struggling to get by. Not in a good place. Disappointed. Frustrated. How about you eighteen years ago? It can seem a lifetime can't it?

We know very little about Jesus's life before he began his three years of ministry. But perhaps that in itself is helpful. He had an unremarkable upbringing and working life. Nothing to write home about. He understands when our lives are like that. Long days, long nights. Good times and bad.

I once commented on a guy spray painting an outside wall, saying that the work looked boring. 'Why?' my then boss asked me, and I couldn't answer. I think I had just seen something routine as being uninteresting. But I know better now. All of life is precious, and at times when work is hard to come by, then a job is very precious indeed. In my time I have worked in a petrol station, two cinemas, a garden centre, and several banks. I've been a Father Christmas, a church caretaker, a creative arts director, a gardener, a mime artist, a movie reviewer, a member of a theatre company and a conference organiser. And unemployed. List them all like this and they are easy to race through. But of course there have been times of loving my work and times of struggling. It's the way of life isn't it.

Jesus never really left his early years behind, they kept emerging in his stories. He talked about gardeners, farmers, sawdust and wood. He talked about parents and money and taxes and building houses. His life became his ministry. All he had lived through were channels of God's mercy reaching out to us. In the everyday. In the times of rest and play, unemployment and work.

His presence right there with us.

What do you think?

....

....

....

....

....

....

....

....

....

....

....

....

....

....

Life

'The best things in life are free...'

The Beatles

Everything upended, the rich poor and the poor rich. The great small and the small great. Fullness discovered in the unexpected places, in the footsteps of an unexpected man. Can't be bought, sold, borrowed or stolen. Instead, a gift. A lens which alters the view of everything; changes reality, history and eternity. God in the dust and the sweat, glory in the gutter, hope nailed to two bits of wood, and breaking free from the tomb-like clutches of death.

'I have come that you might have life and have it abundantly.'

John 10 v 10

* * *

Obed-Edom has a grin as wide as his house.

'You look like you're doing all right,' says Ethan, his neighbour, leaning on the fence.

'Yep, things are going well,' says Obed.

'Business is obviously booming, and your crops are coming up a treat there. What's your secret?'

Obed narrows his eyes, glances down at his feet.

'Well... I suppose it would be all right to show you.'

'Show me? Show me what?'

Obed nods towards his house.

'Got it inside,' he says, his grin spreading just that bit wider.

Obed's wife emerges followed by their four young chaotic children. All of them looking healthier than they had a right to. Ethan whistles.

'Whatever you lot are taking I'll have a bottle,' he says and Obed laughs.

'Can't get it in a bottle,' he says.

Ethan frowns. Shakes his head as they slip inside. The house has grown since he was last inside. An extension out the back and a couple of rooms on the far side.

Obed takes his neighbour up the stairs, a well-dressed servant stops to let them pass. She and Obed exchange a few friendly words before he walks on to a room at the far end of the building. He stops outside the large double doors.

'What's all this about?' Ethan says.

'You'll see.'

Obed-Edom pulls a key from his pocket and eases it into the lock. Twists it and nods as he hears the clicking. He pushes the door open, stands back and offers the way to his neighbour. Ethan steps forward, stops and whistles again.

'You are kidding me!' Ethan says.

Obed laughs and shakes his head.

'That's my secret,' he says.

'Is that what I think it is?'

'Oh yes.'

'But... that thing's dangerous... it kills people.'

'Not in our house. Oh, I was worried at first, but honoured too. When the king asks you to look after the presence of God... it's nothing to take lightly. But you know something? The more we've appreciated it, the more we've cherished it, the more at peace we've become. Having God in our house has changed everything.

Ethan steps forward and reaches out to stroke the Ark of the Covenant. Then he remembers something and pulls back.

1 Chronicles 13

* * *

The Ark of the Covenant was a wooden container, lavishly decorated with gold, which contained the stone tablets of the law along with a couple of bits of manna (the daily bread provided by God in the wilderness). Symbols of God's law, provision and care. When King David attempted to bring it to Jerusalem it all went pear-shaped, resulting in the death of a guy called Uzzah. David then took stock, scratched his head for a while and decided to put some distance between himself and this precious cargo. He called in on a chap called Obed-Edom and left it with him. Obed-Edom was so blessed by God for caring for the Ark that everything about his life blossomed. The presence of God in the heart of his life and home brought renewal and refreshment.

So often the mention of God merely suggests the R word. Religion. When it's not about religion at all. Religion seems to me to be a human construct to keep God safely boxed. To keep him away from the rest of life. From daily reality. And yet that's surely the worst thing we can do. Confine him to a temple or a church. To a Sunday. And perhaps a Wednesday home group. Nothing wrong with any of these as part of the picture. But they are just a part. To offer God our carefully constructed, well-ordered, shiny spiritual bits just won't do.

When folks met Jesus in Galilee they often bumped into him in the street. Without their Sunday best on. When they weren't trying to look good. Jesus did attend the synagogue meetings of course, and he visited the temple. But he usually caused a ruckus when he did so. He wouldn't play the game, stick to the rules. He kept doing and saying things that broke out of the religious framework. He kept mixing God and reality in a way that thrilled the ordinary people and horrified the religious experts.

When Obed-Edom took the Ark into his home, a symbol of the presence of God, he found that his whole life was affected. Not merely the religious bits. The presence of God bled out into every bit of his existence.

What did God do when he wanted to rescue this fallen universe? Made himself human. Not religious. Religion is not really about Jesus. Jesus is about God with us. In everything. After all, he spent thirty years growing up, schooling, working, living, sleeping, eating, sneezing, bantering, playing, sweating, partying, learning, laughing and crying with his family and neighbours in humble, ordinary Nazareth. God in life.

What do you think?

....
....
....
....
....
....
....
....
....
....
....
....
....
....

Blame

All of us tarred with the same brush of imperfection. Falling over our feet. Our tongues running wild like forest fires. Our bootstraps just not strong enough for pulling us out of the mire. On a hill of blame his voice echoes across the centuries. Takes the curse and lifts it from us. Again and again. A gift so precious we could never purchase it. So he does. 'Father forgive them...' The weight lifted, the burden broken. Free.

'I don't condemn you...'
John 8 v 11

* * *

She steadies herself, dusts her dishevelled clothes with hands raw with scrapes and scratches. She can taste grit in her mouth so she turns and spits. She looks to her left. An untidy pile of jagged rocks. Unused now. She turns to her right and sees his words etched in the dust. She looks up, he is walking away now. Upright, calm, focussed. To her left the sight of that gaggle of experts is fading, crooked and hunched as the figures crawl off into the distance. She can still recall their raised fists, primed and ready. And his open hand, offered to her even as he invited the gang to stone her to death. That had been a moment. One of those life-flashing-by-the-eyes moments. Till he had added the killer line. 'Whoever has never broken the law can go first.' For a moment nothing. Her breath held tight between gritted teeth. Her body frozen, torn clothes clutched hard around her. Then that sound. The sweet sound of stones dropping in dirt. Discarded. Unused. One at a time. And the noise of muttering and shuffled steps as the men turned and started to leave. And his open hand offered once more. This time to lift her up, out of her mess. To urge her to start a new life. She frowns. Who is that man? As she watches him walk away she resolves to find out.

John 8

* * *

Another great moment from the gospels. The self-righteous find the ground shifting beneath their feet, the trap they have laid for Jesus springing round to snap them instead. Judging others just comes so easily doesn't it? Second-nature sometimes. I find it so easy to spot the specks of sawdust in the eyes of others, and so difficult to see the chair leg sticking out of my own retina.

And blame seems to be the new game in town now. When things go wrong the solution now is point the finger. I'm so grateful for those who buck this trend. Who dig deep and bring out the oil of forgiveness to lubricate the wheels of life. If getting it the slightest bit wrong is punishable by death then we'd all better start digging graves. Thank goodness for the man who made rescue and forgiveness his life's work. 'I haven't come to condemn,' Jesus told a Pharisee, 'but to save people.'

Sadly the church has not always embodied this attitude. Sometimes it seems as if we are ever ready to pounce on something we perceive to be wrong or unacceptable. To be part of the 'Spot-it-and-stop-it-brigade' to pinch a phrase from Adrian Plass.

Jesus could have looked down from his cross and threatened to sue us all for what we'd done to him. The injustice. The unlawful nature of it all. The bullying and cruelty. But he didn't. Instead, true to his promise about not being here to condemn, he looked at the crowd present there, and at the world across the ages, and prayed, 'Father, forgive them.'

What do you think?

....

....

....

....

....

....

....

....

....

....

....

....

....

....

....

....

....

....

....

....

....

....

....

....

....

....

Treasure

'Buried in a field, till we discover it...'

Matthew 13 v 44

Some of us take years, decades to unearth it, digging a little each day. Some of us find it overnight. Some discover it very early in life, others in the last few minutes. Some of us find it, then lose it again. Some put it to one side then pick it up later. Some never let go. Some don't understand what they have found. Some draw maps for others. We each carry it in the frail containers of our own being. Fragile and damaged. This precious, vital, life-giving treasure.

'For we have this treasure in the cracked pots of our being, so that the light of God can shine out through the cracks.'

2 Corinthians 4 v 7

* * *

It was a hot evening in the field. The sun was gradually dying in the sky – but savouring every last moment as it sucked the moisture from the world below. He sat in the field and looked. The holes surrounded him now, some large and deep – others just handfuls of earth hastily scooped out. The sweat sat heavily on his brow, muddy streaks lined his cheeks and forearms. Where had it gone? Why couldn't he find that place he had marked so clearly only hours before? It had been such a beautiful stone – dazzling. Incredible to find it here amongst the ruts and debris. Like a dream. Perhaps it had been a dream. His mind wandered back over the hectic events. The visit to the estate agent, the sale of his car, the scrambled phone calls, the incredulous response from friends. And all for what? So that he could buy up an empty field and sit in it surrounded by molehills? He stood up and stretched his aching limbs, then stumbled across to the first hole he had dug. Surely he had not been mistaken. Dropping to his knees he burrowed again, a frantic dig, the earth flying around his heels. He stopped. His hand clasped something he had missed earlier. It certainly wasn't his diamond. More like an old piece of coal. He pushed his face close to the handful of rock. In the dying sun something glinted against the black surface of the stone. He twisted it in his fingers. There it was again. A faint flash of beauty that took him right back to the discovery he had made only hours earlier. He stood up and slipped the rock inside his handkerchief. Could this be the diamond he had sold everything to possess?

He would see. It seemed to him very strange, but he resolved there and then to keep it, work at it for a while and hope and pray that one day he would once again see his precious stone...

Matthew 13 v 44

* * *

I wrote the above parable when I was in my late 20s and was pushing the boundaries and exploring a little. I was part of a theatre company and we were using secular songs as backing tracks for our dramas about Jesus. It thrilled me (I'm easy to please sometimes) to be using non-Christian music to communicate stuff about God. It really did. Maybe because I was starting to ask questions about the nature of this God I had talked about knowing for so long. I was moving out of one phase of my faith and into another. And that's partly what this parable is about, discovering that the treasure Jesus offers is not what we first thought.

I link this with Paul's writings on treasure in 2 Corinthians 4. We discover the treasure in the field, and then carry it in our battered, wayward, scarred bodies. In our dysfunctional living. And hopefully, as we do so, folks see God at work, rather than us. We didn't earn that treasure, we didn't get it because we were good people in any way. We didn't inherit it by birth. We have been offered it. Jesus links his treasure in a field masterpiece with another tale about the kingdom of God being like somebody searching for pearls. In other words, as we stumble over the free gift of this treasure, God himself is out hunting for pearls that he deems precious. People. Messy people. People with scuffed knees and bloodied hands. People with dirt under their fingernails. Precious pearls. And as we make a start giving everything for the treasure of a life following Jesus, so God gives everything to rescue us. His whole life. His son. Laid waste on a cross. To pay the price for us pearls.

So back to the treasure. The life offered to us. At first perhaps bright and gleaming and wonderful, but then, over time, we find it more demanding. Not as pretty. A bit gritty in our hands. And unpopular with a whole load of other treasure seekers.

To mix my parables for a moment... remember the farmer in another of Jesus's parables? Sowing seeds, many of which don't take root or produce fruit. Lots fall by the wayside, or get trodden on or eaten up or swallowed by thorns. Some start growing but then fade away. Just a few take root and flourish and bear fruit. This thing is not easy. It takes perseverance.

When I fell apart in the mid-90s I found my faith was not working as it had previously. I had to find another way forward, let God lead me into something new. Having recently read Richard Rohr's book *Falling Upward*, I understand much more of what was going on. Our spirituality changes as we get older. What worked at 18 does not necessarily tick the boxes at 38, or 48, or 78.

This treasure we find is as vital, and relevant and precious as ever. But there is always more to discover, more to learn, as we move on with God.

What do you think?

....
....
....
....
....
....
....
....
....
....
....
....
....
....
....
....
....
....
....
....
....
....

Responsibility

'Tread carefully through this world, with kindness and appreciation in your steps.'

Anonymous

The twin gifts of life and of free will. Offered to us, to see what we might make of them. Great power and great responsibility. In the small acts and the great. To appreciate or disregard, to nurture or neglect. To build up or tear down, to plant or plunder. To sow the gentle, powerful seeds of peace.

'Do your best to mark out a straight path for your feet. Then those who follow you, though they are weak and lame, will not stumble and fall but will become strong.'

Hebrews 12 v 13

'With great freedom comes great responsibility.'

Spiderman

* * *

The friendly old rabbi looks at him with a twinkle in his bushy eyebrowed eye. Your mum and dad will be worried. You know that. Two days it's been now. Jesus frowns. He knows it's the case. But he's certain they'll track him down. Come to the temple and see him in his element. Asking questions, answering questions, listening, learning. These days have been wondrous to him. He'd stay forever if he could. A whole new world. A chance to be here anonymously, no one judging him as Jesus, that boy with the dodgy parentage. Here he can speak freely. Debate, parry, challenge and change. The old rabbi can see. The wrinkles on his brow crease into one another. I don't mind giving you a bed he says, but I have a feeling it's time for you to go home. Jesus senses the man is right. He can't stay here. Not yet. The time is way too early. His boyish impotence tugs at his heart. But he has other things to do. Like learning a trade, building and sweating and experiencing the normalities of life. Puberty and adolescence. Manhood and maturity. Obedience and sacrifice. And so, after one more day of swapping stories and wrestling with theology he'll go home. Let go of these dreams for now.

Luke 2 v 41-51

* * *

In his book *The Wrong Messiah*, Nick Page points out that Jesus's three days AWOL in the temple as a 12-year-old could have been a gateway to a new future as a learned scholar. With the kind of knowledge and wisdom he was starting to display he could have stuck around and got fast-tracked into religious leadership in the temple system. And why not? If he wanted to change the religious corruption why not work at it from the inside? But Jesus knew there was another way. His heavenly father's way. He had to go back to the building site, back to growing up in an ordinary neighbourhood. Back to his earthly father's way. Unprivileged. Gritty. Struggling to get by. Experiencing the kind of days and nights we all experience. Can't have been easy.

It may have been rather tempting to sidestep all that and become the next High Priest. But no. He knew his calling. His father's business may have been about learning and teaching in the temple, but it was also about washing feet, and spending time in the gutters with the overlooked, the unspiritual and the marginalised. Jesus would not use his freedom and power to better himself or make his life easier. He'd come to do something else. Something strange. And to invite others to join him.

In my work, writing and speaking about faith and the Bible, I like rattling cages and rocking boats, I like pushing the boundaries and trying the unexpected. Bending the rules a bit. I like using unexpected stories and films and books and jokes. I have been bored in church most of my life and so I fight that with all my being. I want to make communicating the Christian faith gripping. But I realise I have to be cautious. It may be fine for me but it might not be so for someone else. I'm constantly struggling to work out what unusual ideas might be helpful for others, and what might be plain confusing or misleading. Freedom can be a strange animal. What seems friendly to me might look frightening to others. And vice versa.

My daughter loves horror movies, as I did when I was a teenager. But not now. Not me. I find the stories and images linger in my head and wander the corridors of my brain, waiting to leap out on me in the dead of a sleepless night. To my daughter they are no problem. But to me... I have the same issue with medical dramas. My parents used to watch *Casualty* with no snags at all. But the stories of healthy, happy people ending up sick and sad depress me. So I avoid them. Different things inspire different people.

What do you think?

....
....
....
....
....
....
....
....

Blue Sky Thinking

'I look up at the sky and see the vast work of your hands, and I know you care for us...'

Psalm 8

We open our eyes, to remember, to look up, to see again... this vast and floating world we inhabit. Stopping. Looking. The colours, the shades and hues. The sun chasing the clouds, the clouds fighting back. The moon shooing the day away, the dawn seeping wonder across the fading gloom of night. The quiet shuffling of those white ragged pillows. Unhurried. Dallying, gliding, awesome gentleness. Reminding us we are small yet intensely significant.

Elisha prayed, 'Lord, please open his eyes and let him see!' And the Lord did and the servant saw a vast heavenly army with chariots of fire.'

2 Kings 6 v 17

* * *

The servant shakes in his boots. His mouth moves but nothing comes out. Elisha sighs.

'What is it?' he says, his voice a weary drawl.

'The end,' says the servant.

He's thin, a mere wisp of a man, easily blown over by the winds of change and war and discomfort.

'The end of what?' Elisha bats back at him.

'Us! For goodness sake, you know what I mean. The king of Aram hates you. You keep warning Israel about his impending attacks. Now he's coming with more men than there are grains of sand. To flatten us. It's all over.'

Elisha pushes the servant aside.

'Oh no it isn't,' he says a sudden urgency in his voice.

Elisha looks around for a moment at the surrounding hills. Nods to himself.

'What? What is it?' the servant snaps. 'Are they here already?'

'Don't be daft,' says Elisha and he throws back his head and looks up at the skies. At the heavens.

'Oh Lord,' he cries, so loudly that the servant jumps, 'open his eyes please. Let him see.'

'See wha…'

And so he sees. The servant looks, his jaw drops a mile, and the hills light up. With a sea of fiery chariots as the heavenly army wait there. Divine help.

'See,' says Elisha, 'we're not alone. Now come on, let's go and annoy the king of Aram once more.'

2 Kings 6 v 8-23

* * *

To lift our eyes and see beyond the grey of another day. Not easy that. To get a sense that this is not all there is, in a world where many of the messages coming to us are that this *is* all there is. Abraham was given the sign of a billion stars. Told to look up every night and take strength from those twinkling lights, to be reminded that one day his offspring would be countless. That God was secretly working away behind the scenes on his behalf. That God was on his side. And the world's side. And if he just kept on walking and looking up he'd start to see the beginnings of that. Not so much blue sky thinking for Abe, more night sky thinking.

When Elisha's servant was terrified that an invading army would finish them all off, Elisha lifted his eyes and prayed for better vision for his sidekick. And the scales fell and the servant saw that God was with them in the shape of a much more powerful army.

Oh to see like that sometimes. When the constraints of life promise less, to be able to see that more is still possible. That the God of Abraham and his stars and Elisha and his fiery chariots is exactly the same God right here, right now, closer than you and I can ever imagine. To have our small minds blown from time to time. To remember this jaw-dropping God. Bigger than we might expect, and often, miraculously and no less powerfully, smaller than we expect too.

Like a tiny baby sleeping in the arms of Mary, as his poor mum and dad shuffled into a vast temple, full of doing the business of God. Yet missing this tiny beautiful God when he pitched up. Smaller than they expected. Yet no less powerful. No less able to bring transformation. Thank God for Simeon and Anna, two folks tuned in, two folks with blue sky thinking, two folks ready and able to spot God in a first century babygrow.

What do you think?

....

....

....

....

....

....

....

....

....

....

Failure

'Failure: non-success, non-fulfilment, loss, frustration, life hitting the fan (again), universal, can happen all too regularly.'

A Loose Definition

A shared language we can all speak if the truth be known. We have all walked those corridors of regret, disappointment, questioning and 'if only'. Plans that simply would not be willed into existence. People who could not be steered the way we think best. And sometimes, in the twilight moments of honesty, we have seen these experiences create conversations and build bridges into the lives of struggling others. In the shadow of one moment of historic failure, when loss was transformed into incredible gain.

'When I want to do good, I don't. And when I try not to do wrong, I do it anyway.'

Romans 7 v 19

* * *

The Prodigal's Graveyard

How many are still there, languishing in a never-ending pigsty. Having come so far, so close to home, but for so many reasons they are unable to make the last part of the journey. Sensing that life could be so much more, hearing the distant strains of party music, forever looking down at their appalling rags and imagining a whole new indestructible outfit. But instead they wake each morning, stroke a few pigs, nose about in the trough for some breakfast and tap their feet to that distant beat. Splashing a little more filth on themselves as they do so. Not realising, unaware, that the very troubles they live in are worth so much, become so powerful, when offered to the waiting father. The very things that make the road seem hard, are the very things that could help so many others make the journey.

Luke 15

* * *

I remember hearing Adrian Plass once talk about the way many of us often make day trips back to the pigsty. The demands of being a Christian can weigh heavy sometimes. Even though we know it's not about 'being good' yet, if you're like me, you often feel it is about being good. Often feel as if you are not hitting the mark. And in feeling a failure we can at times feel like veering off the road. Giving up a bit. If only for an hour, or a day, or a week. Yet I also truly believe that failure is a powerful language, one we can all speak. We all know what it is for life to go awry, for plans to not work out, for hopes to be dashed. Again.

And we're not the only ones. Jesus experienced these very things in his time on earth. Philip Yancey once pointed out that one of the reasons Jesus came as a Jewish carpenter was so that God could discover what it is to be human. Don't misunderstand me, I'm not saying Jesus wasn't perfect, but he certainly experienced disappointment, rejection, abuse and frustration. Many of the things which make up our days.

And the one thing he looked when he was nailed up high? A failure. Another failed wannabe Messiah. Come with plans to set the people free and now, like so many other world-changers, nailed up by the Romans. Failed. Thank goodness for that Sunday morning, when the 'failure' walked free and smiled at Mary in the garden.

What do you think?

....
....
....
....
....
....
....
....
....
....
....
....
....
....
....
....
....
....
....
....
....
....
....
....
....

Acceptance

'Seeing the broken, battered prodigal hauling himself up that long, hard road, the kind father ran, and threw his arms around his lost child...'

Luke 15 v 20

An army of prodigals, limping home, day after day after day. Soiled, empty, weary of our own attempts to make life work. Unsure if we'll find a welcome, hopeful for home, longing for love, for open arms, for that voice that says, 'Welcome, you're just what we've been waiting for, come on in. Be at peace. You're okay, let's rebuild, start again.'

* * *

And so he came to himself. Having run out of options, leaked all his energy, exhausted his plan B's. He came to himself. Saw his fears and his foibles and his frustrations. Faced them and unmasked them. Spent himself until there was nothing much left. And so here, surrounded by filth and half-digested food, rats and mouldy scraps, crouching in the cigarette butts of life, he opened his eyes. Took that long walk back to himself. Stopped hiding. Tore down the glossy hoardings of his own making, and let his true nature seep through. Nothing to lose. His rose-tinted glasses lying in jagged shards at his feet. A costly, messy place to be. Yet somewhere in the shadows of his soul he could hear the strains of a new music. Freedom. And the sound of crashing as he threw off the constraints of popularity, peer pressure and pleasing others. And so he came to himself. Recognised the place and named it. Then he stood up and made another journey. Offering himself, rather than the shiny, glossy of idea of who he thought he could be. Trudging, each step heavy with integrity. Back to that risky unpopular place. That house frowned upon by many of his contemporaries. Joked about by the comedians, dismissed by the cynics and shunned by the experts. But nothing of that mattered now. When you've found reality who wants the sham anymore? When priceless treasure is within reach why settle for less? And so he came to himself and he headed down that long road to freedom. Didn't know it yet, but he was headed for the place where welcome was embedded in every particle. Forgiveness in the clean air. Life. Beautifully rampant, extravagantly genuine, wildly colourful. Cup-running-over kind of life. That very thing he'd gone hunting high and low for, waiting for him, at the end of his journey. Returning to that familiar place and knowing it for the first time.

Luke 15

(Inspired by the writings of Adrian Plass.)

* * *

While I was recently reading a part of Adrian Plass's book *The Unlocking*, the line from the prodigal son, *He came to himself* hit me between the eyes. Something about seeing himself for the first time. The gift of being able to perceive reality for a change. What matters. Rather than what we think we should have. Self-realisation, rooted in God's acceptance.

A long time ago now I wrote a a piece of drama called *The Toybox*. You'll find it in here in a few pages time. I was inspired to write it after a vivid and vital summer of discovering that God loved me. It was such a releasing, affirming experience, to know that kind of acceptance. And it was all wrapped up with the thorny issue of self-acceptance. So I wrote about a toy soldier, a clown, a clockwork dancer and a pierrot, who were all struggling to accept themselves.

God welcomes us home as we are, foibles, failings, frustrations and all, and so we are able to accept ourselves a little more. The prodigal knew he was a mess, he could see this after his disastrous adventuring. His brother was in much more danger, he couldn't see himself clearly at all, couldn't imagine he needed to come to his father's party.

Our hearts get hardened don't they? My daughter is six and she has an open, hungry, soft heart. She loves learning and discovering and soaking up all the stuff that comes her way. Sadly I'm not like that. I've learned I need to be cautious. Too cautious at times. I'm stubborn, set in my ways. Defensive. Protective. Life has taught me its hard lessons.

Yet in the 36th chapter of an old battered book called Ezekiel, a prophet makes a promise he heard from God. That it's possible for us to have our hearts softened and opened again. Renewed. And not just once. But regularly. My stony, crud-encrusted, mildewed heart can get a regular reboot. And when I look in the mirror and catch myself looking for all the world like the prodigal's older brother, there is help.

What do you think?

....
....
....
....
....
....
....
....

Songs

'Songs give us voice when our conversation fails.'

Anonymous

We may sing of truth, wonder, struggle, doubt, anger, torment, laughter, praise, awe, faith, adventure, loss, darkness, hope, love, rejection, beginnings, endings, questions, failure, triumph, peace, pain, rest, discomfort, home, exile, deserts, love. So many songs. So many things to say. Music unlocking our spirits, opening the blinds on the windows of our souls.

'My harp plays sad music, and my flute accompanies those who weep.'

Job 30 v 31

* * *

She stares at the harp there. Dumped beside the river. Unstrummed. Unplayed. Looking so wrong. They should be singing, they always sing. No matter what. Songs of innocence and experience. Songs of truth and joy and pain. Songs get them through, enable them to lift their heads and take another step. Yet... their world had been shattered. Torn from its roots. They have been lifted from their home, from their way of life, from their routines of work and worship, food and drink, families and parties. And they don't know where anything is anymore. Especially God. How can he hear their songs now if he is back there in ruined Jerusalem. Their God lying in tatters, mourning amongst the burnt ruins. So what do they sing? What would be the point of strumming her harp now? She reaches for it, runs her fingers over the strings. It's seen better days. Is scarred now from the uprooting. But nevertheless... she begins humming. And the humming becomes playing. And the playing becomes singing. About life and disappointment and fear and loss. And wondering where God is.

Psalm 137

* * *

Do you have favourite music I wonder? Most folks do. Songs that lift them up, help them keep going, bring a smile, or remind them why life is worth living. Or perhaps just spur them on with the hoovering or washing up. I often wash up to the sounds of the 1970s. Everything from Abba and Fleetwood Mac to The Clash, Meatloaf and Bruce Springsteen. I was a teenager back then and they do say that the music from your teens tends to stay with you forever.

I gave it up for a while when I became a Christian, put some distance between me and the past. But a few years later I came back to it. I find it useful in my work now, drawing on the questions posed and viewpoints offered in the lyrics. Recently the film *Blinded by the Light* told the true story of Javed, growing up in Luton in the 1980s, who was inspired by the songs of Bruce Springsteen. The songs helped him to face the problems of racism and misunderstanding.

The Bible has its songbook. We call it the Psalms. And a rum collection they are too. Verses of great wonder and beauty alongside choruses seared in pain, questions, suffering and doubt. Nothing is held back. It's as if the music gives permission for these writers to bring everything to God as worship. Even, as in Psalm 137, a song about not knowing what to sing. The folks have lost their faith and are being persecuted in captivity, so all of this is brought in song. So not having a song gives them their very song to sing.

The Psalms give us permission to offer a broad canvas of worship. Complaint, wonder, tears, laughter, questions, trust, arguments and harmony. These things sit alongside each other and no one makes any excuse. It's the human condition, offered as praise. Offered because that's all we have to bring.

What do you think?

....
....
....
....
....
....
....
....
....
....
....
....
....
....
....
....
....
....
....
....
....

The Toybox

The morning sun streamed through the playroom window, whilst shadows of seagulls glided over the sleeping forms of the toys and animals. In the far corner sat a bright yellow music box – the clockwork kind with a pretty tune and a dancer inside. The dancer was asleep. She always was at this time of day, so too the clown, the soldier and the pierrot. Even the sound of the repairman's boots on the wooden staircase did not wake them all.

The repairman visited the toys each morning, to make sure they were all in working order and good spirits for the children who would be there in the afternoon. The repairman was a good friend and the toys loved and respected him, but not at this time in the morning – at this time they were always asleep.

'Morning toys, it's a brand new day – time to wake up!'

The repairman's voice echoed around the silent room. Not a single toy moved. The stuffed parrot snored and whistled, the teddy bears continued dreaming of picnics, while the rag doll rolled over and collapsed in a different heap. The repairman took a long look at the reluctant toys, gave a heavy sigh, then stepped over to the bright yellow music box in the far corner. Three turns on the brass key and he stepped back to watch the result.

After a second's pause the ticking began, wooden, slow and echoing, like the creak of an old rocking chair. Inch by inch the triangular doors at the top of the box clicked open and with a sleepy, dusty elegance the dancer rose from the old music box. It was the repairman's favourite moment. There was a yawn from the cardboard castle and the soldier sat up scratching his head. The clown and the pierrot flopped out of the toybox and rolled forwards, followed by the crafty fox and the rag doll. Within a few short moments the playroom came to life.

Toys sat up everywhere, stretching their springs and dusting off their wooden legs. The clown produced a toothbrush and happily cleaned his teeth, ears, shoes and armpits with it; whilst the pierrot launched into a complicated routine of stretching exercises. The soldier checked his rifle and his boots before beginning his daily march around the cardboard castle. Three times round and then across the length of the room to the dancer.

The soldier had a soft spot for the dancer, though he would never admit it of course, but it was true that he often chose to march across the length of the room in the direction of that bright yellow music box. As the clown saw this he leapt behind the soldier and crept behind him all the way – until the soldier stopped and the clown walked straight into the back of him, denting his polished red nose. The soldier turned and jabbed him twice – once in the nose and once in the chest. But it didn't hurt, the clown was used to being jabbed by the soldier and he instantly turned his attention to the dancer and began mimicking her slow clockwork turns as he stood in front of her – which only made the soldier even more angry, while the dancer looked a little confused.

The soldier was about to jab the clown a third time when the dancer made a rather bigger movement than was usual for her, stretching her arm its full length in order to bash the clown full in the face, squashing his nose into a funny pancake shape. The soldier nodded approvingly, the dancer giggled nervously – the clown just fell over. At this point the pierrot, who had been watching from a distance came leaping over and seeing the clown lying so still he sadly produced a handkerchief and draped it ceremoniously over the clown's face. The dancer's smile turned to shock, the soldier wasted no time in joining her inside the box to comfort her. As the two figures continued their mournful, clockwork routine the handkerchief suddenly shot off the clown's face in a sudden blast of air, and the clown himself jumped up and pulled the largest face he could possibly muster at the other three. The poor dancer's shock turned to horror. It was all too much for her. The repairman cleared his throat to interrupt.

'I wouldn't mind, but we have the same old routine every morning!' He scratched his head, 'come on, line up – repair time.'

The soldier stepped smartly up, but the clown pinched his place at the front of the queue, until the soldier jabbed his rifle into the clown's neck and sent him packing.

'Ah soldier, any complaints this morning?' asked the repairman.

'There's always something to complain about in this place!' the soldier snapped back. 'Everything's so disorganised – especially him!' He jabbed his rifle at the clown again. The clown stuck his tongue out and pinged the soldier's braces.

The repairman was used to this attitude from the soldier.

'Oh dear, what is it this time – stripes fallen off? No... braces snapped? No... ah I know – a hair out of place!'

'Nothing so trivial! It's my saluting arm, hasn't been oiled in weeks!'

The repairman laughed, 'Oh if that's all it is, that's easily remedied.' The repairman's oil gun squeaked three times and the soldier stamped off saluting over and over again just to make sure.

'Clown – what's your problem?' asked the repairman.

The clown smiled back. 'By dose is binching be.'

'What?'

'It's by dose – it's binching be,' said the clown.

The repairman peered down the clown's throat. 'Sounds like your tonsils, or maybe your trousers are too tight!'

'Doe!' squeaked the clown, 'It's by... ' He yanked at his dented red nose. 'It's my nose – it's pinching me! The solider jabbed me again. And the dancer bopped me. It's not fair.'

'Oh come on, I hardly think the dancer would get the better of you, anyway... you'll live,' the repairman took the battered nose and slipped it into his pocket, 'I'll take this to the Toymaker - he'll fix it, just don't do any sneezing in the next twenty-four hours!'

The clown looked as if he might just sneeze right then, so he quickly clamped a hand over his face and waddled over to the toybox.

'And what about you, pierrot, what's wrong with you?' The repairman walked over and sat next to him on the floor.

'Nothing,' said the pierrot and he turned away.

The repairman was not convinced. 'Nothing?'

'Nothing your bag of tricks could fix anyway.'

The repairman leant over and tightened his shoelace and thought for a minute.

'The Toymaker might be able to help, though,' he said.

For a while the pierrot said nothing. Then:

'Oh... I just don't fit in here, I'm not like the others.'

The repairman looked perplexed and asked him what he meant.

'Well, take clown, he's always making people laugh, cracking the right jokes, telling the right stories – no one laughs for me. And dancer, she's so elegant and talented, she knows all the right steps, never puts a foot wrong – me I just bungle around.' He sighed, 'And then there's soldier – so smart and disciplined, he's always trying to straighten me out. I want to be happy and popular and smart but I can't. I just don't have what they've got, I try but I can't.'

The repairman listened quietly and nodded. He thought for a few minutes then decided what to say. 'Listen pierrot...'

'Look at the time!' The soldier thundered suddenly, 'it's nine o'clock! Time to work for the Toymaker!'

The pierrot buried his head. 'Oh great! Late again...' he said and he ambled off to do some exercises.

Of course, the toys didn't really have to work for the Toymaker, their job was only to be there for the children, but the soldier had long-since established his work policy for the first hour of each day and everybody else had believed and followed him.

The repairman took a step back and perched on the windowsill taking in the scene as the toys began their routines. Clown produced a magic blue hat and managed to pull four chickens, three rabbits and a plastic bicycle from it. Soldier took his gun to pieces and carefully cleaned each part, taking the trouble to see that the dancer was all right every couple of minutes. She was very happy of course, doing pliés by the side of her bright yellow music box. Pierrot quickly grew tired of his usual routine and crept away from his chair to watch the clown pulling a series of objects from his hat. Pierrot then found his own blue hat from the toybox and reached in to pull out four chickens, three rabbits and a bicycle – but all he got was a shock when his hand shot out with two hairy spiders sitting on it.

The repairman continued to watch the pierrot as he then turned to follow the soldier who was practising a few marching steps. Pierrot pushed back his own shoulders and tried to march upright in a similar fashion but he couldn't see where he was going and walked right into the toy mousetrap which bit into his foot and made him shout rather loudly. Pierrot hobbled away and turned his attention to the dancer, and on seeing that she had left her music box to try a few steps across the floor, he climbed inside and tried some elaborate clockwork pirouettes. There was an almighty crash and the whole of the playroom turned to look as the pierrot tripped over his own feet and came tumbling out of the box headfirst. The soldier marched over and scolded him, the dancer looked very upset indeed. The repairman decided it was time for a break.

'Okay, toys, it's wind-down time!'

'OHH!'

'No arguments, clown, you've already got bags under your greasepaint. No more work until the children come this afternoon.'

With a few more complaints the toys wandered back to their boxes. The repairman strolled over to the pierrot who was holding his injured foot.

'It's no good, I'll never be like them...' pierrot was saying, nursing his bruised foot, 'I tried, I really tried...'

'Pierrot, are you ready to listen now?' the repairman asked, 'have you finished dashing around trying to be something you're not?'

The pierrot looked as if he wasn't sure what to say.

'Pierrot, let me show you something,' the repairman went on, 'take a look at clown now.'

They looked across the room, the clown was trying to entertain the rag doll with a bag of tricks, but she looked quite bored and soon walked away. The clown shook his head and suddenly looked very sad, until one of the bears went past and the clown put on a grin and did a ridiculous tap dance in his massive red shoes.

'You see,' said the repairman, 'he's always happy and joking on the outside because inside he's lonely. Behind his smile there's a broken heart. And look at the dancer, she's always practising those perfect movements of hers because she's frightened of standing still. She has to keep moving, she's afraid of what might happen if she stops. And then of course, there's soldier...'

The pierrot looked up at the cardboard castle and got quite a shock, for the soldier was standing without his hat and gun just staring at his reflection in the window. There were two very large tears dripping down his cheeks.

'Yes, he is very disciplined, on the outside, because inside he's falling apart. That's why he's trying to tidy everybody else up, he's a little ashamed of himself. You see, pierrot, they're hurting too – just like you. Only they're not yet as honest as you. But the Toymaker does know about these things and he does want to help... which reminds me, I forgot to give you this when I came in this morning.'

The repairman reached into his overall pocket and pulled out a beautiful, shiny, black ruffle.

'What's this?'

'It's a gift, from the Toymaker.'

'But why,' asked pierrot, 'what did I do?'

'Nothing. He just wanted to say that he loves you. You see he made you a pierrot, not a clown or a soldier and that's exactly the way he wants you. Here, take it and wear it for him. Be a pierrot for the Toymaker, not a clown for somebody else.'

Pierrot didn't know what to say to this but he watched as the repairman slipped outside and shut the door quietly, leaving the toys for another day. Then he took the ruffle in his fingers and felt it with pride and excitement, and with nervous fingers he clipped it round his neck and then sat nursing his battered foot. But the tears that ran down his face weren't there from the pain, they were from something else...

Printed in Great Britain
by Amazon

17765215R00102